CHANGING THE SYSTEM

SAGE HUMAN SERVICES GUIDES, VOLUME 24

SAGE HUMAN SERVICES GUIDES

a series of books edited by ARMAND LAUFFER and published in cooperation with the Continuing Education Program in the Human Services of the University of Michigan School of Social Work.

A **SAGE** HUMAN SERVICES GUIDE **24**

CHANGING THE SYSTEM
Political Advocacy for Disadvantaged Groups

Milan J. DLUHY

Published in cooperation with the Continuing Education Program in the Human Services of the University of Michigan School of Social Work

SAGE PUBLICATIONS   Beverly Hills   London

For information address:

SAGE Publications, Inc.
275 South Beverly Drive
Beverly Hills, California 90212

SAGE Publications Ltd
28 Banner Street
London EC1Y 8QE, England

Printed in the United States of America

Library of Congress Cataloging in Publication Data

Dluhy, Milan J., 1942-
    Changing the system.

    (Sage human services guides ; 24)
    1. Handicapped — Government policy — United States — Citizen participation.
2. Handicapped — Services for — United States — Citizen participation.
I. Title.   II. Title: Political advocacy for disdadvantaged people.   III. Series.
HV1553.D57   362.4'0456'0973   81-14331
ISBN 0-8039-1726-0 (pbk.)   AACR2

FIRST PRINTING

CONTENTS

Preface

This book is about political advocacy and how to become better at doing it. Since disadvantaged groups are generally unrepresented or underrepresented in the political process, much more political advocacy on their behalf is desperately needed. Ironically, one of the most frequently ignored facets of practice in social work and the human services is political advocacy. Political advocacy on behalf of the disadvantaged is not unprofessional, politics is not always "dirty," and the use of power and influence to achieve worthwhile objectives is not a waste of time. On the contrary, a professional commitment to social change in today's world requires that myths and stereotypes such as these be buried once and for all.

This book takes the position that successful political advocacy is worthwhile, it can be learned, and knowledge about it is essential to what competent practitioners in social work and the human services should know. It is also worth emphasizing that the ingredients of successful political advocacy for disadvantaged groups apply broadly regardless of whether you are advocating for the poor, elderly, youth, disabled, mentally ill, the battered, or the infirm. That is the case because, for the most part, the political process deals with such groups in very similar ways. Consequently, we have a lot to learn by simply comparing notes as to what has worked and not worked and why.

This book is aimed directly at people who currently are in some way involved in serving disadvantaged groups in our society. It is necessary neither to have had a great deal of experience nor to be very sophisticated in political advocacy to understand the content presented herein. In fact, the presentation of material is organized in a way that lends itself easily to widespread use by those people serving disadvantaged groups who have either not seriously considered getting involved in political advocacy in the past or have had very negative or unrewarding experiences when they have been involved. It is probably safe to assume that some people are already good at political advocacy and may not know why, while others are motivated to do better but do not know where to start. In either case, a careful reading of the following pages will provide you with plenty of insight as well as practical suggestions. The material which is covered can easily be used when working with community groups, agency staff, interagency staff, or even as part of an ongoing staff development or in-service training program. Special attention is paid in the text to illustrating how the material can be used with audiences such as these.

Finally, I would like to thank the many practitioners and students who have been exposed to the material presented in different chapters of this book over the last three years. Many of the ideas, illustrations, and exercises have come directly from them and in this respect, I believe, the reality base of the material has been enhanced substantially. Political advocacy for the disadvantaged is as important today as it has been in any other period of American history, perhaps even more. The hope is that more well meaning and humane people will see the necessity of performing this type of service on behalf of the disadvantaged and that this book will in some way contribute to helping these people perform that service.

Chapter 1

BECOMING A COMMITTED
POLITICAL ADVOCATE

We have at one time or another all been frustrated, angry, and even alienated by the political process that we participate in as we seek to influence and shape the direction of policy in this country. Some burn out and withdraw as a result of this frustration, others very pragmatically conclude that their energies are being wasted because of the lack of any clear or tangible results that come from this involvement, and still others choose only token participation in this process because they have long ago concluded that active participation does not make any difference in terms of what is or is not done for various disadvantaged groups in this country.[1] While I share all of these views to a certain degree, *my overall perspective is that better, more focused, and responsive policy will not be developed and implemented without the determined and consistent involvement of political advocates representing disadvantaged groups in the political process.* To withdraw from that process or to be minimally involved only allows others with perhaps very different values and ideas about these groups and their needs to prevail. We all hear complaints about these other people, but successful political advocates need to do more than just complain, they must adopt a proactive stance toward policy and the political process which produces it. *The underlying theme of this volume is that successful political advocates must take a proactive stance toward policy and the political process on a regular and ongoing basis.* As such, they must be willing to understand more thoroughly the political process they work in, the tasks that must be carried out to influence the development of better policy, the specific skills that are attendant to those tasks, and the personal and organizational roles and strategies that are the most likely to achieve desirable policy outcomes for the groups they represent. Thus, proactive political advocates must *continually* develop new skills and acquire new knowledge while at the same time sharpening old skills and reinterpreting old knowledge. Political advocacy for a few comes easily in the sense that they are successful even though they give little forethought to what they are doing. We all know people like this, and we have much to learn from them. However, most of us, and I include myself in that list, must think more consciously about what we are doing and whether our actions, behaviors, and strategies are appropriate given the political process and its constraints. Therefore, it is necessary to constantly assess in a critical fashion how we go about seeking to influence policy and whether we could do it better.

The purpose of this volume is to provide a framework for understanding the political process as it relates to the development and implementation of policy. The use of this framework is intended to introduce some to the field of political advocacy for the first time and to sharpen the understanding of those who have been involved in such work over the years but who have been frustrated and ineffectual.

The overall framework to be introduced and discussed in Chapter 2 will be more useful if it is understood in the context of a philosophy of social change. We all have some ideas about how social change does and should occur in our political system and these ideas in most instances strongly influence how we personally choose to be involved in that system. For example, if we are fatalists about social change and only believe it will occur as a result of some revolutionary or more dramatic set of actions, then we may be very likely to play only a very limited and peripheral role in the political process, since only a major event or political movement will make a difference in terms of social change. On the other hand, a more optimistic view of change may argue that change is always occurring and those involved in promoting it will, in the long run, stay with it and apply continuous pressure. This view implies a more proactive, ongoing role for individual people.

To take a step back, we may say that most political advocates have some kind of philosophy or orientation toward social change. At a minimum, this philosophy includes some ideas about the magnitude of change as well as the time span over which it occurs.

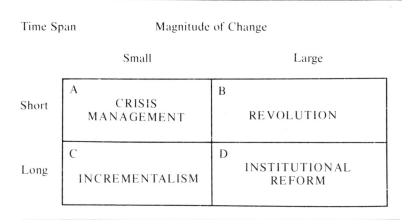

Figure 1 Theories of Social Change

Figure 1 graphically portrays the magnitude and time dimensions associated with change. Cell A indicates a *Crisis Management* orientation toward change in the sense that small changes are always occurring as a response to individual crises. These changes or responses to crises are not well thought out since the principle is that any response is desirable or good as long as it occurs quickly and responds on the surface to the immediate crisis or need. People who share this view of social change are likely to move from one crisis to another, putting a Band-aid here or there, and then moving on to the next injury or crisis. I would characterize political advocates who share this orientation toward social change as "fire-fighters." "Fire-fighters" burn out, get tired, and need a rest; and after a while, they may withdraw from the political process entirely out of sheer exhaustion.

Cell B suggests a more *Revolutionary* orientation toward change in that only major or macro restructuring of institutions, groups, and ultimately systems is acceptable. There is little patience with the Band-aid approach of those having a Crisis Management orientation. Rather, the Revolutionary wants substantial (large) change; and he or she wants it now, not later. Minor tinkering with policy, for example, is unacceptable and fruitless given this orientation. Therefore, political advocates who share this orientation toward social change are generally branded as "Radicals" since they seek major and fundamental change and want it in the short not long run. The most realistic consequences of this orientation are that "Radicals" either withdraw because of their frustration or their inability to see major change occur over the short run or other actors in the political process ignore their arguments and see them as unrealistic and unfeasible and thus keep them on the periphery of the political process where influence is hard to exert.

Cell C characterizes an *Incrementalist* orientation toward change in the sense that while change at any one point in time appears small, if one looks cumulatively over a period of time, the changes begin to add up. These changes are not necessarily just immediate responses to crises but, rather, they are small adjustments to policy which require a great deal of bargaining, accommodating, and negotiating between participants in the political process. Change is therefore small, difficult to achieve, and generally consistent with past precedents. Political advocates who view change in terms of Incrementalism can be referred to as "Pragmatist-Brokers" who are continuously involved in applying pressure, moving issues along, adapting the system to new needs, and doing all this in a realistic and pragmatic context which stresses that change must occur step by step, not in single leaps or bounds. "Pragmatist-Brokers" stay involved in the political process over long periods of time. These people are a major force to be contended with, since, to be effective, they must be involved in and knowledgeable about all that is happening in the long-term political process.

Cell D represents the most sophisticated (from my perspective) orientation toward social change. There is recognition that change must occur realistically over long periods of time and that the system cannot handle, nor will it tolerate, major restructuring in short time frames. On the other hand, this orientation stresses that if a lot of small changes are added up over time and directed toward some fundamental goals for restructuring or redesigning institutions or systems, then *substantial* (large) change can indeed occur. Incrementalism often appears to ignore any long-run view or perspective on the substance of what is to be changed. The frequent criticism of this orientation is that it lacks any long-range purpose or direction.

Correspondingly, those with an *Institutional Reform* orientation have a long-range perspective. For example, Incrementalism as an orientation may cause political advocates to tinker endlessly with the school system in an effort to get it to respond to the needs of runaway youth or status offenders but there may never be any larger view or perspective on what a restructured school system might look like so that small incremental changes might be directed toward that ideal. In contrast, those with an *Institutional Reform* orientation have a clear idea of the end in mind, and they seek to develop a series of minor changes in a way that leads in the long run toward major change and redesign.

Those sharing this view will be referred to as "Committed Political Advocates." They are patient, realistic, knowledgeable about the political process, involved on a regular basis in it, and committed over the long run to a major restructuring of the institutions and systems serving disadvantaged groups. By definition, they are committed to political advocacy as a life-time career. They do not withdraw, they do not sporadically participate, they do not respond in an ad hoc way to problems — rather they are regular, ongoing participants in the political process with a vision of the future. In short, they are leaders among their peers and within their profession. Decision makers and the public turn to them for advice on issues affecting disadvantaged groups. And they are the people these groups most respect as their advocates.

STOP AND THINK

See how many "Fire-Fighters," Radicals, Pragmatist-Brokers, and Committed Political Advocates you can identify, then analyze what personal, social, and organizational characteristics they have.

Being a more successful political advocate is the topic of this volume. A thoughtful and intelligent way of becoming a more successful advocate is to first reexamine one's philosophy or orientation toward social change. It is the assumption that an Institutional Reform orientation toward social change produces a "Committed Advocate" with the highest probability of achieving desirable change for disadvantaged groups. The *Framework* presented herein is an attempt to identify the theories, concepts, skills, and knowledge necessary to become that sort of a person. We all, at one time or another, have been "Fire-fighters," "Radicals," or "Pragmatist-brokers"; and it is not that these kinds of people are unnecessary in shaping policy in a positive direction, but rather that a larger number of more mature, committed, and dedicated political advocates need to work a lot harder to acquire the range of knowledge and skills necessary to be successful than do "Fire-fighters," "Radicals," or "Pragmatist-brokers." But then, that is the price one pays to become a more successful political advocate for disadvantaged groups.

NOTE TO USER OF THIS VOLUME

This volume is directed toward those people who currently are in some way involved in designing, managing, and evaluating programs serving disadvantaged groups at the state and local level. I refer to these people as "program people" for a lack of a better term. Since "program people" are the primary audience, the volume is designed in a way that people who have had limited and perhaps frustrating experiences with the political process can understand the steps necessary to become more successful political advocates. The volume is not designed for the experienced and sophisticated political advocate who has been involved in this game for many, many years. Accordingly, the format of the volume is to lay out theory, concepts, application, exercises, and resources aids in a way that is easy to follow. A glossary of terms is included at the end to assist in the overall understanding of the material presented.

A major caution to remember in using the volume is that it should not be used as a "cook book" that is read but not discussed. Many of the concepts need to be more thoroughly exemplified, challenged, and validated; and this is hard to do without interacting with other people who are willing to discuss the contents of this volume.

It is therefore recommended that the material presented should be used when working with community groups, agency staff, inter-agency staff, or as part of an ongoing staff development or inservice training program. Chapters 1 and 2 should be read by everyone interested in political advocacy. Each subsequent chapter presents a separate part of the framework and can be used individually with groups such as those mentioned above. For example, if the volume is being used to help orient community groups toward how to build more effective political coalitions at the local or state level, you would have the participants read Chapters 1 and 2 plus the chapter on coalition building.

On the other hand, if you were going to use the volume to help agency staff understand the policy development process more completely, you would have the staff read Chapters 1 and 2 plus the chapter on the Policy Development Process. At the end of each chapter some suggestions for the potential groups that might be particularly interested in the content presented in that chapter will be mentioned along with some ideas about how this content might actually be used in a training or discussion situation. In short, this volume is designed and written for the practitioner. The volume gives practitioners suggestions for how to master this content and in doing so how to become a more successful political advocate.

Learning that has *direct* application to your job is not always readily apparent in this volume. Tolerate some concepts and ideas that may on the surface only have *indirect* application to your current job. The framework provided is a way of thinking critically about political advocacy for disadvantaged groups more than anything else. It cannot be learned in one sitting or reading. The framework should be used over and over again and tried against reality as much as possible and changed when it is apparent that it does not fit. In the end, the framework allows you to take a step back from the day-to-day hassles of boards, committees, police, caseworkers, other agencies, the government, and so on and judge realistically and critically whether you can improve your ability to affect policy in a positive way.

NOTE

1. The reference to groups in this volume is to target groups like youth, elderly, ex-offenders, battered women, disabled, and so on which generally are not very well-represented in the political process. Therefore the perspective presented throughout is how to become a better political advocate for disadvantaged groups. Accordingly, illustrations will be used in this volume to show a more general application of the concepts to as many disadvantaged groups as possible. The reader should substitute his/her special target group when considering the material presented in each chapter.

REFERENCES

BRAGER, G. and S. HOLLOWAY (1978) Changing Human Service Organizations. New York: Free Press.
KADUSHIN, A. (1978) Child Welfare Strategy in the Coming Years: An Overview. Washington, DC: Government Printing Office.

REIN, M. (1976) Social Science and Public Policy. New York: Penguin.
RIVLIN, A. (1971) Systematic Thinking for Social Action. Washington, DC: Brookings Institution.
ROTHMAN, J. (1974) Planning and Organizing for Social Change. New York: Columbia University Press.

Chapter 2

UNDERSTANDING SUCCESSFUL ADVOCACY

Successful political advocacy is contingent on the selection of an appropriate strategy — one that maximizes the use of available resources to achieve policy objectives. Historical events, the state of the economy, and the mood of the country or community are things generally outside the control of the political advocate. They frequently must accept these constraints as they pursue their policy objectives. However, if we take these kinds of things as given, there is still a substantial amount of control over behavior, resources, and strategy that the political advocates can have as they make their case. In short, political advocates may have little control over the unemployment rate in their state or community, but they may have a lot to say about the range of programs available to the families and individuals affected by the economy if they are able to make their case successfully. These are areas where the results of their political advocacy are likely to be seen.

A careful review of policy areas like child welfare, aging, education, veterans affairs, income maintenance, community development, and social services (Title XX) over the last 10 years demonstrates that successful political advocates in these respective areas take into account certain critical elements as they make their case and plan their strategy (see Dluhy, n.d.). These critical elements generally determine success or indicate failure in the political process. The important issue after these elements have been identified is to determine those that are most important or that combination of elements which consistently leads to success. This is a difficult assessment to make.

The following discussion provides an overall *framework* for understanding successful advocacy. *The framework is composed of the four critical elements most often found in the policy-making process when political advocates are making their case.* Analysis of these elements will usually help you understand why a political advocate has been successful or unsuccessful. Throughout the volume, and whenever you have an example of successful or unsuccessful advocacy, you should run it through this framework to determine which element or elements were critical to success. It is in this way that you can build on the framework and integrate it into your own actions, modifying it as need be to make it more realistic and useful. (See exercise at end of this chapter.)

The critical elements of the framework can be illustrated initially by posing a set of four questions about the activities and behaviors of political advocates regardless of the arena they are working in. To what extent do the political advocates:

(1) appeal to the objective needs of clients in the given circumstances or situations?;

(2) manipulate successfully the value symbols of the dominant actors or groups involved in making policy decisions?;

(3) propose policies (or change) in such a way as to maximize the policy's impact on a range of important beneficiaries (clients)?;

(4) have organizational strategies capable of influencing the outcomes of policy debates?

In short, these four questions are premised on the understanding of how to: *appeal to objective need; manipulate values; design policy for relevant target groups; and build political organizations supportive of policy positions.* Although it would be hard to imagine successful political advocacy that ignored any of these elements totally, it might be reasonable to expect that successful political advocacy might emphasize one element over another depending on the circumstances and availability of resources. Illustrations below will make this point clearer.

APPEALING TO OBJECTIVE NEED

As political advocates make their case, they are frequently called upon to demonstrate as clearly as possible the needs of their client.[1] In demonstrating need, they must be clear and concise about it and whenever possible document the need with statistics, research, case records, surveys, and so on.

More important, they must not only be able to demonstrate the need of their client but also be able to *compare* their client with other clients and show why their client is worse off and in more need of support in a policy sense. Political advocates for the elderly who are poor, for example, can easily show the shrinking income and diminishing purchasing power of the elderly over time; and they do just this with statistics wherever possible. However, they are even more effective when they contrast the circumstances of elderly with those of other age groups in society (i.e., 30-35, 36-50, and 51-60). The figures on income and purchasing power always make the elderly who are poor appear to be in worse shape relatively.

Veterans are another case in point. Figures on unemployment, alcoholism, drug abuse, and mental illness for veterans are always higher than for nonveterans of the same age category. Youth unemployment in the inner city, the school drop-out rate of a community, the incidence of sexual abuse among female runaways, and the periodic psychological crises experienced by "hard-to-place kids" who go from one foster care setting to another are further examples of appealing to objective need. The political advocate quantifies the need of his/her client and then compares this client with a client whose needs are relatively less problematic. One must, of course, have the figures to use this approach as well as a comparable group so that the differences can be made as dramatic as possible.

STOP AND THINK

Identify the statistic about your client group which works best for you. Who do you compare your client group with? Could you be more effective in this area?

Many "program people" would like to make this kind of case but agency records or follow-up studies may not be available to provide the proof. For example, careful data collection on runaways locally is necessary across the country before national organizations can make their case with Congress, the Department of Health and Human Services, and the Office of Management and Budget with more confidence and effectiveness. Generally, figures on delinquent youth are more readily available than those on runaways. Data collection problems also exist for such groups as battered women, ex-offenders, displaced workers, abused children, and so on.

To repeat, political advocates emphasizing this element of the framework must be careful to make sure they have the data and the relevant comparison group or their opponents will be able to destroy their case. Political advocates should not use this appeal unless they have done their homework and done it well. In the political process, decision makers cannot allocate money to all groups who demand it, so they will have to establish criteria for allocating money at some point. If the criterion of objective need is well-defined, it can be used to counter the political clout (or voting strength) of persons not interested in this population. It increases the likelihood that the political advocate will be successful.

In contrast, if one were advocating for senior citizen centers (open to all seniors regardless of income), family counseling programs for middle-class families, or general revenue sharing for suburbs, the case would most likely be based on political clout (or voting strength) since it would be extremely difficult to make the objective need case, as described above, for those kinds of clients. The challenge for those representing disadvantaged groups is to clarify the need or problem, collect information on the extent of the need or problem within the group, and then compare the disadvantaged group with a group which is not as disadvantaged.

MANIPULATING VALUES AND SYMBOLS

Political advocates frequently represent their clients in the political process. The language they use to refer to their clients is critical. The words they use may raise fears or touch the hearts of their audiences. These words represent values to other people, and it is necessary to consider whether these words affirm or reinforce acceptable and widely shared values, whether they activate new (but positive) values, or whether they either affirm or activate negative or deviant values. Data or statistics may be unnecessary in many circumstances if the political advocate is able to manipulate through language or symbols the right set of values for his/her audience. Of course, the elderly are "deserving." Who can be against "crippled children?" Is not "family treatment" preferable these days to "individual treatment?" *The caution and care that a political advocate takes with language cannot be overemphasized.* The wrong words, or the use of words which are too low key for the audience, may make the case even harder to make. Words evoke passion in people. They move people to action. Never doubt the importance of the message.

For example, if you were seeking funding from traditional (in a value sense) community groups or churches for a runaway home, would you refer to your clients as "kids," "runaway kids," "troubled teens," "youth from families in crisis," "victims of society," "abused youth," "estranged youth," or "youth in crisis?" If you were seeking to get to people's conscience and perhaps build on a sense of guilt, one set of names would be preferable to another. Often pathological descriptions of clients, as those above, are more effective with certain audiences. One caution: While certain audiences want data and more neutral language, others want and need the dramatic language. Attention to "value manipulation" with different audiences through use of language will pay off in making successful cases.

Finally, there are circumstances when values ought to be affirmed or reinforced, other times when values ought to be left ambiguous, and still other times when new values ought to be appealed to. It is easy to see that the value of family stability and maintenance ought to be affirmed or reinforced whenever possible when making the case for runaways — thus, the appelation "youth from families in crisis" mentioned above. However, when you do not have or do not know the appropriate values to appeal to, then you should be value ambiguous or neutral and avoid value connotations. Otherwise your opponents will use these values against you. Using pathological connotations with professional clinicians, bureaucrats, or some funding agencies often does not work since they want data, based on research studies; and if you overdo it, they will refer to you as hysterical or accuse you of wearing your heart on your sleeve. Appealing to a new set of values may occur in situations where old values no longer work. Many think that characterizing elderly as a wasted economic resource is a new value appeal that may work in the future since it indirectly relates to an old value, economic efficiency. The effective advocate must be on a continuous search for fresh and innovative value appeals.

STOP AND THINK

Take the client group you work with and identify the most (and least) effective way of referring to them. Could your value appeal be better? How?

Successful political advocates are always aware of the values they are appealing to. They modify their language and value appeal according to the audience they are dealing with. This is a simple point; but a reanalysis of agency documents, board minutes, and previous political conversations may reveal your failure on a regular basis to manipulate values according to the intended audiences. It would be a good habit to keep a log on important political conversations and look carefully at all agency-written documents over a period of time so that you could examine critically the language you have been using when advocating for your client.

DESIGNING POLICY FOR RELEVANT TARGET GROUPS

When a political advocate is putting together a policy proposal or recommendation for the actors in the political process, a fundamental design question must be addressed. Should the proposal be aimed at geography and numbers or targeting and visibility? For example, with child abuse programs, should the shrinking program dollars be spread thinly across the United States so that as many programs in as many states as possible are funded or should these dollars be concentrated in a few, very visible programs where the problems of child abuse are most severe and the chance of program success the highest? This is a real dilemma because spreading the money out increased future political support for the program while concentrating it demonstrates success and reinforces the appeal to objective need mentioned earlier.

The spreading out syndrome can be found in programs like Child Welfare Services, Title XX, HUD "701" planning programs, Title I educational Aid, Community Development Block Grants, The School Lunch Program, and the Food Stamps Program, to name a few. Alternatively, the targeting and visibility strategy can be found in the areas of child abuse and neglect, teenage pregnancy, crippled children services, handicapped educational programs, E.P.S.D.T. (Early Periodic Screening Diagnosis and Treatment, of children from low-income families), and so on. The challenge is to narrow the focus, concentrate the resources, target the clientele, and prove success from a programmatic standpoint rather than spreading resources out and building a political base. To get caught between either of these approaches is to fail in a political sense, since it is difficult to make a case for something that is neither politically popular nor successful from a program standpoint.

Consequently, designing a successful policy proposal means that careful attention needs to be paid to this issue. Either approach can be successful but do not get caught in the middle. Emphasize one or the other.

STOP AND THINK

Given your experience, have you been more successful in the long run when you targeted program resources or spread them around?

BUILDING ORGANIZATIONAL SUPPORT

A political advocate may have: the statistics on his/her side; the proper value appeal; and the most appropriate policy design and still fail. Failure may be due either to the lack of political support or ineffectual political support for a certain policy.

This element will be discussed in the chapter on coalition building; but the key point is that successful political advocates constantly struggle to create, build, and then maintain political organizations which will effectively support their policy positions. These political organizations are more powerful if they: represent most, if not all geographic areas;[2] are comprised of large memberships; have distinctive ideologies and clear value positions; are easy to mobilize in policy debates; have large amounts of tangible resources at their disposal; and possess leadership which adroitly represents the organization's position in policy debates.

Finally, an organization that is stable over time and can deliver regularly is most successful. Shortcomings in any of the areas mentioned above mean weaker organizational support. Some unions, business groups, professional groups, public interest groups, and age-related groups historically have approximated this ideal. It is common knowledge, for example, in Washington, D.C., that the United Auto Workers, the National Association of Manufacturers, the American Medical Association, Common Cause, and Children's Defense Fund are illustrative of some of the most successful political organizations in national politics.

While all political advocates may not have such organizations backing them, in the long run, they would do well to approximate and work toward the most stable political organization as possible. Ad hoc organizations with high turnovers in membership and leadership frequently are ineffectual in the political process because they basically are not in it. The ideal may ultimately be to control the political process itself in the policy area of concern. We may criticize the oil companies, unions, and teachers; but we are aware that they control the political process which produces policy affecting them and in this sense we are using them unconsciously as a model.

STOP AND THINK

Identify both a good and a bad example of political organizational support. What made these examples successful (or unsuccessful)? Analyze key characteristics of each.

CONCLUSION

The framework for successful political advocacy consists of four critical elements that must be dealt with in the political process. It goes without saying that if you have the statistics, right value appeal, proper policy design, and stable political organization you are more likely to be successful than if you do not. The middle-class elderly, the veterans, and the physically handicapped, to name a few, have mastered these elements quite well. But what about political advocates for youth, battered women, the rural poor, and frail elderly women living alone in the inner city? *If you are advocating for such groups, you should adopt at a minimum two principles as they relate to the framework presented.*

---

1. **The Flexibility Principle**

   Make sure you vary your case to fit the audience. Diagnose the audience carefully and decide which of the elements to emphasize. Do not use the same argument (element) all the time, vary it to suit the circumstances. Be prepared to make four, not one presentation(s) if you are unsure of what the audience wants and needs.

2. **The Overcompensation Principle**

   Play to your strong suit whenever possible. If the audience is receptive to a value appeal and you do it well, why bother with anything else? Overcompensate by doing what you do well first and then making other kinds of cases if you can and need to. Expending resources in areas you do not do well in is foolish and wasteful.

EXERCISE

The following exercise can be used with a wide variety of audiences and has broad application. Depending on the size of the overall group and time limitations, pick about four people to make brief presentations (15 minutes). Each person is asked to exemplify both a successful and unsuccessful strategy that he or she has used. They are to use the four elements of the framework in assessing these strategies. Participants not presenting should critically analyze each presentation in light of the framework and its elements. The group leader should emphasize the application of the framework and its individual elements, while stressing the overall importance of the flexibility and overcompensation principles.

In larger groups (over 12) a panel (of 4) format is desirable. In smaller groups (under 12), it may be possible for everyone to be a presentor. In either case, a group leader is needed to facilitate discussion and connect the practical experiences of the participants with the framework. *Make sure everyone has read the chapter and understands it before the exercise is begun.* The purpose of the exercise is to make sure that participants understand that different strategies are used and these strategies depend on who the political advocates are, what resources they have, and how they perceive their respective audiences. In any event, critical assessment of previ-

ous behavior is to be encouraged. With luck, most of the participants will
say at the end of the exercise that if they had it to do over again, they would
now do it differently. Or, if they had to do it over, they would emphasize one
element of the framework more than the others.

NOTES

1. Client refers broadly to the disadvantaged group or groups that the advocate is
representing.
2. This depends on whether one takes a community, state, or national perspective.

REFERENCES

ADAMS, B. (1979) "The limitations of muddling through: Does anyone in
    Washington really think anymore?" Public Administration Review 39 (6).
CLOWARD, R. and F. PIVEN (1977) "The acquiescence of social work." Society
    14 (2): 53-63.
DLUHY, M. (n.d.) "Comparing political strategies used by groups representing the
    disadvantaged." (unpublished)
DLUHY, M. (1981a) "The changing face of social policy" in J. Tropman et al. (eds.)
    New Strategic Perspectives on Social Policy. Elmsford, NY: Pergamon Press.
DLUHY, M. (1981b) "Policy advice givers — advocates? technicians? or prag-
    matists?" in J. Tropman et al. (eds.) New Strategic Perspectives on Social
    Policy. Elmsford, NY: Pergamon Press.
GILBERT, N. and H. SPECHT (1974) Dimensions of Social Welfare Policy. En-
    glewood Cliffs, NJ: Prentice-Hall.

Chapter 3

POLITICAL ISSUES AND VALUES

BACKGROUND AND ASSUMPTIONS

One of the most difficult tasks of the political advocate is to make sure that the issues being debated in the political process are clearly stated and presented in a way that other participants in the political process understand them. We often hear, after hours of discussion, the questions, "Will you please repeat what the issues are?"; "Will you clarify what we are talking about?"; "What are we voting on?". The task of issue framing becomes critical to the overall policy debate, and successful political advocates need to develop skills in framing issues in a common language.

Closely related to the task of issue framing is clarifying the underlying value systems or ideologies of the participants in the political process. Many participants rarely speak in the debates, others make only token comments, while still others say one thing but mean something else. The problem for the political advocate is to figure out the perspective of others so that the political advocate's case can be made more successfully. *This perspective will be referred to as that person's ideology – the set of values that people have about how the political system operates and should operate and how that system ought to respond to problems.*

Diagnosing this underlying ideology is not easy and often it takes many interactions with other people plus careful and reflective analysis of their motivation and behavior over time. The payoff is that clarification of ideology allows strategy to be more efficiently focused by the political advocate. One, for example, would not want to be making a radical appeal to a conservative for too long since it will be a waste of time and perhaps counter-productive in that the conservative may eventually respond negatively if pushed too hard.

When ideologies and the value systems that comprise them clash, we have a value dilemma. The skillful political advocate will recognize what these dilemmas are and have techniques for resolving them; or if that is not possible, withdrawing from these situations to avoid further damage.

Framing issues clearly, diagnosing the underlying ideologies of participants in the political process, and developing techniques for resolving value dilemmas are all important tasks that political advocates need to be able to perform skillfully. In making their case, these tasks are closely *associated with the critical elements of the framework – appealing to objective need and manipulating values and symbols*. The assumptions of this chapter are that political advocacy will be more successful if:

(1) the advocate is able to continually clarify the issues and keep the debate from straying from his or her central concerns

(2) the advocate is able to surface, understand, and respond to the various ideological stances of the participants in the process

(3) the advocate is able to develop techniques for resolving value dilemmas when they occur.

The reasoning behind these assumptions is that we should wherever possible make things explicit and not leave them implicit. The more explicit and clear the debate is, the easier strategy can be designed. Correspondingly, leaving things implicit or unclarified only raises the frustration level of the political advocate and makes strategy development more difficult and problematic.

CONCEPTS AND ILLUSTRATIONS

ISSUE FRAMING AND CLARIFICATION

There is a need for common language when policy debates are occurring. Most issues that you are likely to encounter in these debates can be categorized and placed into four areas. It often takes work to clarify an issue into one of these areas but with practice you will be able to do it quite easily. These four areas are:

(1) *The Basis of Allocation* — Who is eligible for the program? Are we trying to expand, contract, or maintain the people eligible for the program? Who do we want the program to serve? All of these questions are ones of allocation.

Thus, issues like changing income eligibility guidelines for Title XX services, changing the definition of what a runaway is, or changing the kinds of organizations that can receive or be funded under a particular program are all allocation issues.

(2) *Type of Social Provision* — Having decided who will be the beneficiary of the program, the question is what will you give that person, group, organization, or community? Will it be money or direct payment? A voucher to purchase services in the community? Counseling? Job training? Or what?

Issues like allowing programs to contract with other agencies for services, allowing states to reimburse agencies for consultants under Title XX, or allowing local departments of social services to contract with various programs for services for youth in foster care are all provision issues.

(3) *Strategies for Delivery* — Having decided who the beneficiaries of the program are to be and what you will give to those beneficiaries by way of money or service, the question is how will you be organized to deliver those services? What organizational structures and personnel arrangements will be used? Will neighborhood clinics be used? Will centralized multiservice agencies be used? Will highly centralized and managed systems be used?

Most questions of organizational design, management, information systems, and personnel arrangements are delivery issues.

(4) *Methods of Finance* — What will be the sources of funds for the program? Is a local or state match required? At what rate will reimbursement be set? Any issues related to the funding of a program's activities and who is to pay are essentially ones of finance.

While these four categories may appear deceivingly simple, you will find it essential to take issues within your agency, community, and state and classify them as either allocation, provision, delivery, or finance issues. Then a common language can be established. Your task is to fit issues into one of these areas and clarify for the participants that you are dealing with that kind of issue. You must be able to pinpoint in the policy debates the kind of issue you are most concerned with, repeat it, and get others to agree that this is, indeed, the issue. This is hard work but a clearer agenda and a more focused strategy is possible if issues are framed properly.

STOP AND THINK

Take four or five issues that you have been involved with over the last year and try to frame them as either allocative, provision, delivery, or finance issues. Would others agree with your classification?

IDEOLOGICAL CLARIFICATION

There are three basic ideologies in the American political system about how that system ought to operate and how it should respond to problems. These are portrayed in Figure 2 and illustrations from the youth area are indicated in the last column. You should be able to substitute illustrations relevent to the populations on whose behalf you are advocating. Go over the columns a number of times. See if you can identify people you have encountered in the political system who share each of these ideologies and then see if they support solutions such as those in the last column. The point of ideological clarification is that if people use a set of values to interpret most things, then their solutions will generally be the same regardless of the issue. This allows you to predict responses by understanding ideology. Ideology rarely changes, so that if you carefully diagnose the ideology of a participant in the political process, you can adapt your case to respond to their concerns or at least clarify who your friends and enemies are.

RESOLVING VALUE DILEMMAS

Frequently value conflicts occur between key actors, organizations, or systems. The political advocate may be asked to help resolve these conflicts. If you are clear in your own mind about what these values are and what part they play in someone's overall ideology, then you can work on developing skills for resolving these conflicts. Three

Ideology	Overview	View of Political System	Perception of Problem	Solutions
RADICAL	Wants basically to restructure the system, its institutions, and its processes	Inherently corrupt, designed to benefit upper or dominant class, political system merely reflection of economic system	Problems are inevitable and will always be there because the system is corrupt.	Must change the system or restructure it entirely.
				Create alternative living situation for runaway.
LIBERAL	Wants basically to marginally change system, institutions, and processes.	Basically accepts political system and believes it occasionally must be changed or adapted if problems occur.	Imperfections in the system that need to be corrected, but patch up system, don't radically restructure it.	Government corrects imperfections in system.
				Get runaway into family therapy counseling program, etc.
CONSERVATIVE	Leave system, institutions and processes alone, but change individuals and their behavior.	Basically accepts political system and wants to preserve its features	Failures in individuals, not the system therefore, problems are those of individual, not system.	Keep government role limited and stress change in individuals.
				Blame runaways and get them back home and into school.

FIGURE 2   Ideological Perspectives

suggestions for resolving value dilemmas when they are encountered are:

(1) *Use the averaging or moderation principle* — Be clear about where both sides are and split the difference. Compromise but only go halfway. Let the other side know this. A lot of labor negotiations near the end follow this pattern. A lot of work is necessary on just where each is in terms of values. Be patient. Work hard.

(2) *Value Ambiguity or Avoidance* — It becomes clear to you that if your values are clear to other participants in the process, you will lose politically. Therefore, you let them use and think their values are being accepted, while making sure the substance of any agreement benefits your position. Give them the satisfaction of language and symbols, but make sure the consequences of the agreement clearly benefit your position. This is deceptive and manipulative, so watch out. You cannot later throw this in the opposition's face or you can never do it again. You must be content with policy success even though appearances suggest otherwise.

(3) *Value Appeal and Affirmation* — Count your votes ahead of time. If you have a majority, reinforce the values of your supporters. Move them to action. Ignore the opposition. Do not put them down. Your strategy is to play your strong suit and appeal to the values of your supporters. Expend energies on stimulating your supporters. In this sense you are not resolving the dilemma, except by winning the debate.

You will use all these techniques in a value dilemma situation since the nature of the debate may change rapidly. Be aware of what you are doing and change strategies when necessary.

One example may be illustrative. The dilemma is that the Title XX system in your state may want to make sure state-funded programs (yours) are being used only for the intended beneficiaries. They value efficiency (make sure only those who are eligible are receiving services) and accountability (being able to track program dollars).[1] On the other hand, your program is committed to honoring the confidentiality of the client and his/her family so that the program does not discourage clients from entering their system. The question is how to preserve confidentiality while complying with efficiency and accountability. Following the above discussion, the suggestions would be to:

(1) bargain with state agency so that names, addresses, and personal identifying information is not given but cases and other facts are summarized in tabular or a neutral recording fashion

(2) use false names, addresses, and personal identifying information under the assumption they will never check, or array information so that it would be impossible to trace it to any individual client

(3) take the state to court, appeal your case, fight the process until they give up.

Obviously, the third suggestion is very costly, the second very deceptive, and the first, time consuming. You will have to decide which risks you are willing to take.

EXERCISE

The following exercise can be used with a wide variety of audiences and has broad application. The issue raised revolves around the choice that a particular program has between merger with another program, program expansion, or program termination. The example used relates to two programs dealing with youth. However, you could easily substitute two programs related to the elderly, children, battered women, and so on, depending upon the group discussing the content in this chapter. Have the participants read the hypothetical case a number of times and then in no more than two pages respond to the tasks at the end of the case. They should do this only after they have read the chapter. The group leader then selects (depending on time) at least *three* people to present their solutions. A general discussion should follow in which the importance of issue framing, diagnosing underlying ideologies, and resolving value dilemmas is stressed. The purpose of the exercise is to get participants to see the application of the concepts presented.

THE CASE

Background

Community Setting	*Program No. 1*	*Program No. 2*
400,000 population	Runaway House	Teen Counseling Center
unemployment rate of 12%	uncertain funding	permanent funding
predominantly conservative ideology	10 years old; short-term treatment; small client load; no more than 15 runaways at any one time	15 years old; emphasis on long-term treatment; visible in community, especially with school system

runaways originating from neighborhood in inner city	75% of runaways are local inner city kids from black or low-income families or both	middle-class clientele, caseload about 100 at any one time
churches mildly interested in runaways	main interactions of program have been with juvenile justice system in past	director is an organization builder and wants to broaden services and clientele served
conservative school and legal system	low visibility in community	

Problem and Issues

Program No. 1 is losing 40% of its funding base and it has, for the last six months, been unable to find another source or sources to make it up. The accountant and the director have concluded after financial analysis that the short-term treatment of runaways will not be possible any longer given current resources. Therefore, they conclude that the agency can follow one of three paths:

(1) merge with Program No. 2

(2) add new programs emphasizing youth employment, teenage pregnancy, or long-term care

(3) merely liquidate their assets and go out of business.

Tasks

Pick either the merger, program expansion, or program termination option (pick only one).

Indicate, using the issue clarification language, four likely issues that may surface in the debates. Frame these issues as one of allocation, provision, delivery, and finance.

Identify the underlying ideologies for each of these issues. For example, what would the liberal, conservative, and radical position be on the four issues associated with merger, expansion, or termination?

Demonstrate how you would suggest resolving the major ideological and value dilemmas presented by each issue by choosing one of the three approaches mentioned in this chapter.

NOTE

1. Issues such as these apply to many programs. The case is only illustrative.

REFERENCES

CHURCHILL, S., et ai. (1979) No Child is Unadoptable. Beverly Hills, CA: Sage.

COCHRANE, C. and D. MEYERS (1980) Children in Crisis: A Time for Caring, A Time for Change. Beverly Hills, CA: Sage.

DLUHY, M. (1979) "Design and delivery of social welfare services: Politics and issues at the local level," in G. Tobin (ed.) The Changing Structure of the City. Beverly Hills, CA: Sage.

TROPMAN, J.E. (1978) "The constant crisis." California Sociologist 1 (1).

TROPMAN, J.E., et al. (1976) Strategic Perspectives on Social Policy. Elmsford, NY: Pergamon.

Chapter 4

THE POLICY DEVELOPMENT PROCESS

BACKGROUND AND ASSUMPTIONS

Political advocates all work with the policy development process. More successful advocacy is achieved by understanding the nature of that process and how it works. This chapter focuses on three central ways in which political advocates can acquire knowledge about how the process operates and functions. *First,* political advocates need to understand the *major norms* which explain how the policy development process operates in practice. *Second,* political advocates need to be able to identify and understand which model of *decision making* is being used so that they can determine the major access points when seeking to exert influence. *Third,* they must be familiar with how to specifically *identify* which people to approach when they seek to make their case. That is, they must be able to identify the most powerful and influential actors so that they get to the right people.

Ultimately, political advocates must be able to understand the norms of the process, how decisions are made in that process, and which people they should approach to make their case. Put another way, unless the political advocates understand the game they are playing and the key actors they are interacting with, they cannot exercise influence and make their case effectively. You cannot have influence until you have access; and you cannot know the points of access without knowing the rules or norms of the game. Each piece of knowledge is central to successful political advocacy.

Strategy is most effective if it is based on a clear understanding of the policy development process that the political advocate is working in. You cannot understand a football game without a program or scorecard, just as you cannot understand policy outcomes without a blueprint of the process which formulates them.

CONCEPTS AND ILLUSTRATIONS

NORMS OF THE POLICY DEVELOPMENT PROCESS

Over the years, I have observed a number of "truisms" about the policy development process. These might be called the norms of that process, and as such they must be dealt with by political advocates working in that process. Ignoring these observations when developing strategy means overlooking some fundamental aspects of the process. Look them over. Examine them in light of your own experience. Try some examples of your own and see how well they fit. Review some political strategies you have used recently to see whether you have taken these truisms into account or not.

The five observations or truisms are:[1]

(1) *Advocacy, not analysis, is the major source of new programs and policies.*

   (a) Programs and policies seldom arise from research or problem analysis.

   (b) Programs and policies come into existence because some group or individual effectively advocates the desirability or necessity of the program or policy.

   (c) While crises provide convenient occasions for advocacy, they are not the sole occasions for effective advocacy.

   (d) Programs and policies conceived in advocacy relationships may often use studies or research for justification or legitimization.

   (e) Programs and policies are usually enacted quickly with temporary coalitions. Coalition politics is more important than research and analysis.

(2) *Program and policy design is atheoretical.*

   (a) Programs and policies are rather ambiguous regarding objectives or at least conflicting in purpose.

(b) If any theory exists, it is that there is a belief that forcing a "match" by state and local governments or private/ voluntary agencies will encourage or guarantee program achievement.

(c) Most program and policy designs are atheoretical in terms of performance; they do not really know what to expect.

(d) The assumptions on which most programs and policies are designed have never been proven or tested out empirically ahead of time.

(3) *Program design is political and pragmatic.*

(a) Absence of theories does not imply absence of organizing principles.

(b) The legislature and bureaucracy share an interest in being responsive to their respective constituencies or clientele.

(c) Programs and policies usually cover in their distribution of benefits enough congressional districts or states to generate enough political support for passage and continuation (spreading out syndrome). In the case of states or communities it would mean coverage of the entire geographical area.

(d) The political incentives for being responsive and spreading program funds out means that the real program is money and how it is distributed, rather than any comprehensive approach to a particular problem.

(e) The predominant approach to program and policy design follows the "see what happens" syndrome; do something, appropriate the money, look at it in two or three years, and, depending on who testifies, modify or adjust the program or policy so as to maintain a working coalition which supports it.

(4) *Successful policies and programs generate their own constituencies.*

(a) Bureaucratic program managers buy support for their programs and policies by spreading out the funds to clientele groups and constituencies; this simultaneously allows bureaucrats to cultivate the support of the legislature in the next budgetary or reauthorization cycle.

(b)   The influence of the "Iron Triangle" (that is, bureaucratic program managers, legislators, and clientele groups) is the driving force behind the continuation of most programs and policies.

(c)   Programs and policies which encourage inherent political alliances are popular and difficult to terminate (at the national level, some examples would be the HUD 701 program, Hill Burton, Impact aid, community mental health, Title I education funds, Title XX social service grants, and community development grants).

(d)   Program consolidation or reorganization of programs are opposed by everyone except those interested in economy, efficiency, and management. Everyone else protects their turf or domain.

(5)   *Program and policy goals are inherently unstable over time.*

(a)   Since problems and legislatures change periodically, it is no surprise that program activity is governed by the search of bureaucratic managers for ways of generating continued public and legislative support.

(b)   Alliances change, degrees of advocacy change, but the basic norm is that goals can shift to accommodate working political coalitions which maintain programs over time.

MODELS OF DECISION MAKING

While the previous section identified the major truisms which characterize the policy development process, it is important to take the next step and identify more specifically how decisions are made and by whom. This more detailed information on decision making allows political advocates to identify more specifically key access points or places where they can make their case. For example, if a closed-and-behind-the-scenes, decision-making process is being used, then a political advocate testifying before a congressional committee in an open forum would be wasting time and exercising an ineffectual strategy.

On the other hand, if the decision process was largely internal to the bureaucracy and its procedures, the adroit political advocate would have to have access to that process. Or finally, if the decision making was occurring in a variety of places, some open and visible and others closed and behind the scenes, then the political advocate would have to be present at and part of a whole series of bargaining and negotiation sessions. The three most common models of decision making are presented in Figure 3 along with illustrations and some obvious implications for strategy.[2]

The way to use Figure 3 is to read and apply as many personal examples as you can to each model of decision making and then examine how well you accommodated your strategy to the decision-making process being used. Having access to a small number of key elites, having access to an organization's agenda-setting process, and being part of and having access to a complicated set of bargaining games is quite different situations for the political advocate. The advocates' challenge is to identify, at any one point in time, the decision-making model being used so they can develop their strategy and make their case to the right people. These models suggest overall access points for the political advocate. The challenge for the political advocate is to perceive the model of decision making being used accurately.

STOP AND THINK

Take a recent decision of importance to you. See if you can reconstruct the way in which the decision was made. Which model best fits your example? Did your strategy take into account the model of decision making that was used?

IDENTIFYING KEY ACTORS

After determining that the major access points are either a small set of key elites, a small number of organizations and their leaders and members, or a large number of elites who are either organizational spokespeople or speaking largely for themselves, political advocates must decide *specifically* who to approach to make their case. They may have a general idea from understanding the decision-making models but now they have to approach specific people. *People have political power if they have the capacity to change the behavior of other people in the direction they intend. Therefore, we want to locate people who have large amounts of political power.*

Characteristics	I. Rational Actor	II. Organizational Process	III. Bureaucratic Politics
General Portrayal	Decisions are deliberate choices of leaders or elites — they game things out and seek to maximize their own values given constraints and without direct input of masses or interest groups — anticipated reactions are critical.	Organizations have substantial lives of their own, decisions are outputs of large organizations functioning according to standard operating procedures which are patterns of behavior which are routinized over time. Focus on organizational maintenance over time and less on individuals.	Decisions consist of a whole series of bargaining games that go simultaneously; key individuals are involved in different bargaining games where each is relatively autonomous. Results or outcomes of bargaining are not intended ahead of time but result of bargaining, accommodation, compromises, etc.
Visibility of Actions	Low	Medium to High	Varies — at critical stages, low and behind closed doors, occasionally overt if actors seek popular support.
Range of Actors Involved	Limited to key elites (inner circle).	Organizational elites and occasionally membership.	Multiple elites depending on bargaining games, and how big issues are.

FIGURE 3   Three Models of Decision Making

FIGURE 3 continued

Characteristics	I. Rational Actor	II. Organizational Process	III. Bureaucratic Politics
Decisional Constraints	Few — except as perceived by elites. No direct constraints.	Moderate — but know ahead of time the organizations's position. Predictable constraints.	Many depending on actors involved, many different bargaining positions.
Information Requirements	Low — may use data but do not need information from other actors or groups.	Moderate — but it is biased to fit position of organization.	High — need knowledge of other actors and their positions.
Outcomes	Optimal choices	Marginal adjustment or Incrementalism (Organizational maintenance)	Satisfying — accept feasible not optimal solution
Some Illustrations	Foreign policy International security Macro economic policy	Social Security Education Housing Income Maintenance Social Services (Title XX)	Civil Rights /Race Relations Energy Taxation Health Insurance
Implications for Strategy	Must have access to key elites to have influence	Must be able to build and shape an organization's position.	Must be on the spot and willing to be involved in continuous bargaining and negotiation.

We know powerful people change the behavior of other people by using *inducements* (i.e., money, jobs, contracts, votes, and basically any material benefit), *threats* (i.e., violence or the threat of violence), and *persuasion* (i.e., appealing to shared values or norms). But are there some easy ways that we can identify these powerful people or actors? Four helpful ways are:

(1) *Formal Job or Position Held* — Focus only on formal heads of organizations, boards, or commissions under the assumption that they have access to large amounts of political power.

(2) *Reputation for Power* — Ask others familiar with the decision-making area who generally exercises power when decisions are made. These people may or may not be formal leaders. They may often hold no formal job or position, yet be very powerful. These people would be the "hidden elite."

(3) *Personal/Issue Power* — Observe personally, over time, the decision-making process and determine who seems to be persuading others the most and whose position usually wins out. This is usually done through experience and participant observation.

(4) *Veto Power* — Observe or ask others familiar with the decision-making process who normally is able to veto key decisions or keep things off the agenda indefinitely. These people exercise power in a negative as opposed to a positive way. They only respond to initiatives of others.

You can use all of these techniques if you have time and, if they all show up identifying a core set of people, then you should have confidence that you are directing your case correctly. Relying on only one technique can be dangerous, since you will always miss a few people and these in practice may turn out to be the most critical people for your group and its interests. The safe thing is to compare notes and techniques with other advocates to see if perceptions of power and power holders match up.

EXERCISE

Have all participants take one policy development process they have been involved in recently. This should be one involving an attempt to change policy or legislation outside of their agency or organizational setting. Review the truisms identified earlier and assess which of these were and were not present in their example. Then, decide which model of decision making was used in the example and detail how well it fits one of the three models by following the figure presented in this chapter. Have them recall which decision makers were approached and why (which technique they used). Finally, have participants in a panel format (three or four people) critically assess how well the strategy they actually used took into account the norms, models, access points, and key actors presented in this chapter.

This assessment is meant to provide after-the-fact insight into what went wrong or could have been done better. Some may not have had enough experience to do this. They should work with a more experienced person. The group leader should take responsibility for facilitating the discussion. The purpose is to have participants connect norms, models, access points, key actors, and the strategy they used. Many will find their knowledge thin in some of these areas. That should encourage them to seek more information the next time they plan strategy.

Finally, if the participants generally lack experience with the policy process and find it hard to connect their experience with these concepts, rely on the experienced in a panel format to share their perceptions with the full group. Here the panel should be carefully selected and asked to lay everything out for the rest of the participants. In contrast to other exercised in this volume, only the experienced will find it possible to complete the entire exercise. On the other hand, the less experienced can learn from the panel if their "stories" are vivid, easy to relate to, and put in the context of this chapter.

NOTES

1. Many of these truisms are adapted from Anton (1980). His study, while based on an investigation at the national level, has many analogies at the state and community level as well.
2. The models are adapted from Allison (1971).

REFERENCES

ALLISON, G. (1971) Essence of Decision. Boston: Little, Brown.
ANTON, T.J. (1980) "Federal assistance programs: The politics of system transformation" in D. E. Ashford (ed.) The Politics of Urban Resources. New York: Methuen.
DYE, T. (1978) Understanding Social Policy. Englewood Cliffs, NJ: Prentice-Hall.
GILBERT, N. and H. SPECHT (1974) Dimensions of Social Welfare Policy. Englewood Cliffs, NJ: Prentice-Hall.
HECLO, H. (1977) A Government of Strangers. Washington, DC: Brookings Institution.

LAUFFER, A. (1978) Social Planning at the Community Level. Englewood Cliffs, NJ: Prentice-Hall.

LAUFFER, A., et al., (1977) Understanding Your Social Agency. Beverly Hills, CA: Sage.

LINDBLOM, C. (1968) The Policy Making Process. Englewood Cliffs, NJ: Prentice-Hall.

SEIDMAN, H. (1970) Politics, Position, and Power. New York: Oxford University Press.

TROPMAN, J. E., et al. (1976) Strategic Perspectives on Social Policy. Elmsford, NY: Pergamon.

Chapter 5

UNDERSTANDING DECISION MAKERS

BACKGROUND AND ASSUMPTIONS

Once political advocates have identified the key actors or decision makers that they should be making their case to, using the procedure suggested in the last chapter, the question is, how should the case be made? The answer to that question should be based, at a minimum, on an assessment of the decision-making styles and orientations of the actors involved and their information needs, along with a careful assessment of the political advocate role you have decided to play when interacting with them. Each is important for a different reason. The decision-making style of the actor is the process that a person uses to make decisions, the things he or she emphasizes in making decisions. For example, what are the informational needs of the decision maker and in what form should information be presented to them? Finally, political advocates, after analyzing the decision maker's needs, must decide how to come across as a person to the decision maker. They must select the role they seek to play when they provide information to the decision maker. Successful political advocates must consider these key variables when designing a strategy.

Unless a careful analysis of individual decision maker's needs is made and the appropriate role chosen for interacting with that decision maker, successful political advocacy cannot be accomplished effectively. Issues may be framed properly, ideological diagnosis of actors may be accurate, and the relevant access points and key actors may have been determined, but you may still fail if you do not pay attention to the more specific and, often, idiosyncratic needs of these decision makers. Which role should be played is also essential. Attention to these kinds of details pays off. Ignoring the decision maker as a person could be a foolish mistake.

CONCEPTS AND ILLUSTRATIONS

DECISION-MAKING STYLES AND ORIENTATIONS

There are three basic decision-making styles that can be found among key actors in the policy development process. The critical distinctions among the three decision-making styles can be understood by focusing on their primary emphasis. For example, above everything else, the *rational/deliberative* emphasizes, and values highly, information that has been collected, analyzed, and interpreted according to certain methodological norms and procedures. Even though these kinds of decision makers may have little time to read and process information, they will be looking for information presentations that follow the things mentioned in Table 1.

Since methodological adequacy is so important, it is easy to see why decision makers with this style use data in a highly instrumental way — that is, it is the careful collection and analysis of data in a scientific way which primarily determines the decision maker's position on an issue. Decision makers may still need to have documents that are concise, readable, dejargonized, brief, and available in time, but the information should be presented in a way that *emphasizes methodological adequacy* for those decision makers who process information in a more rationalistic/deliberative way.

Table 1 includes some speculation on the possible background characteristics of decision makers with this style. They are offered in a suggestive way so that one can get a feel for the types of people who may be likely to have this information-processing style. However, the description of the style and its focus is more critical to this discussion, while the potential background characteristics which may explain style are intended to stimulate more thinking about the topic. In the latter case, one striking thing about the backgrounds of people with rationalistic/deliberative styles is their general lack of practical first-hand experience with the issues, programs, or policies being considered.

The *pragmatic/incremental* style first and foremost emphasizes and values the feasibility of the recommendations offered. Because this style stresses such things as getting things done, moving ahead, keeping the agenda alive, "what will go," and so on, data and analysis are usually used to legitimize an organizational, political, or personal position. Data are not the driving force for these decision makers but rather it is getting something done. Therefore, compromises on research design, a focus on only a few realistic options, and a willingness to use whatever data are avilable, regardless of their reliability and validity, are reasonable adjustments to make if decisions have to be made in the short run.

Methodological adequacy is replaced by feasibility, pragmatism, and getting things done. Again, some speculative background characteristics of this style are offered in Table 1. One critical point on these characteristics is that extensive practical experience in decision making would seem to drive out more scientific and rationalized ways of processing information because the longer one is involved in day-to-day decision making, the more likely one is to see that process as highly personal and political in nature.

Finally, the *emotional/ideological* style is one which most clearly represents the commitment to action. If something needs to be done, do it. Do not wait for the methodological proof. Make your arguments persuasive. In this context, data and analysis may be secondary to making a convincing argument. Therefore, appeal to values, make issues visible, focus clearly on the option or recommendation; and do all this in a way so that something happens today not tomorrow. When the problem or need is compelling, data and analysis as well as the careful exploration of the feasibility of the recommendations are secondary to action. You may have observed that people at the top and bottom of organizational hierarchies (not middle) are most likely to use this style — those at the bottom because they are close to the action (people, clients, programs, problems) and those at the top because one of the reasons they are there may be due to their longstanding commitment to a cause, a problem, a clientele group, and so on.

In summary, Table 1 differentiates three different information-processing styles and orientations. Political advocates as they prepare documents and make their case orally to decision makers need to accommodate their presentations not only to the time constraints faced by decision makers but also to their information-processing

TABLE 1 Summary Characteristics of Decision Making Styles and Backgrounds

Decision Making Style	Background Characteristics	Summary Characteristics of Style
Rational/Deliberative	Academic or disciplinary training Minimum practical experience Mid-level organizational position Appointed rather than elected	*Emphasis on methodological adequacy of presentation* Instrumental use of data Logical or internal consistency in presentation Quantification emphasized Research design approximates experimental design Comprehensive alternatives analyzed Analytical/technical experts valued
Pragmatic/Incremental	Eclectic training/experiences Considerable practical experience High level organizational position Either appointed or elected	*Emphasis on feasibility of recommendations* Data used to legitimize position External political support assessed Both quantitative/qualitative data desired Eclectic flexible research designs Only realistic, feasible alternatives analyzed All types of advice evaluated
Emotional/Ideological (Surprise or Accidental)	Social Work, Law, Gerontology, Child Development, etc. Practical experience varies considerably (novice or expert) Low or high level organizational position Either appointed or elected	*Emphasis on the immediacy or action orientation of recommendations* Persuasiveness of argument is critical, data secondary or irrelevant Appeal to values, consciousness-raising, dramaturgy Qualitative data preferred Research design irrelevant Only one or two alternatives considered seriously Moral, ideological spokesmen or experts valued

style. Successful advocacy follows accurate diagnosis of decision maker needs.

STOP AND THINK

Using Table 1, identify the decision-making styles of as many people as possible that you are familiar with. Are the background characteristics represented by each style similar?

SELECTING THE APPROPRIATE POLITICAL ROLE

The conventional view of the concept role is utilized here. Thus, a role is a set of prescribed behaviors and relationships that are in accordance with the expectations that others have toward that role and any incumbent of that role. By referring to role, the focus is on the range of expectations surrounding the giving of advice (or making your case). *Analytically, three possible role types are presented: the dramatist, the technician, and the pragmatist.*

At this point, the issue of expectation is separated for the purpose of discussion into personal role expectations and social role expectations. The former refers specifically to the person giving the advice or making the case while the latter refers generally to the decision makers, the organizations, and the parts of society who are receiving the advice. This discussion focuses primarily on the role expectations of the people performing the "advice-giving" function. How do they perceive themselves? What, for example, are their expectations as to whom they should be giving this advice? Are they clear about the intended audience?

"Advice givers,"[1] whether consciously or unconsciously, organize their work in the policy world according to the variety of audiences they deal with on a day-to-day basis. And while it may be true that quite diverse audiences having very different amounts of specific knowledge, expertise, and experience in a particular area will read or be exposed to the work of the advice giver, it is not necessarily true that the advice giver is organizing and presenting his/her work for all of these audiences. It is more realistic to say that advice givers have primary and secondary audiences in mind as they do their work. For sake of argument, it might be possible that some advice givers can accommodate all the relevant audiences, but as you have probably observed, personal role expectations differ enough across advice givers that distinct patterns according to intended audiences can be identified and classified.

The tripartite categorization of roles introduced above allows some of these patterns to be matched with their associated audiences. For example, the *dramatists* would perceive their primary audience as: clientele directly affected by (or benefiting from) a particular policy, organizations or bureaucratic units who have as a part of their mission serving the clientele of the policy directly, and authoritative decision makers who historically have consistently supported and been predisposed toward that clientele in a political sense.

The dramatist would also pay somewhat less attention to secondary audiences like: other clientele closely identified with these organizations or bureaucratic units and authoritative decision makers who have supported these other clientele in the past. *The important point to emphasize about dramatists is that they primarily aim their work at only a subset of audiences that they might be interested in influencing.*

The subset is composed of people, organizations, and decision makers already predisposed toward and supportive of the affected clientele or direct beneficiaries of the policy. Secondary attention is paid to people, organizations, and decision makers identified with or supportive of other clientele groups who are closely associated with or aligned with the primary clientele group. In short, the dramatist's personal role expectation is that when they do things like research, analysis, memo writing, testimony preparation, and so forth, on problems of disadvantaged groups, they will prepare written documents or give oral presentations that are aimed at audiences already supportive of their work.

This has many implications for the nature of the documents prepared or the oral presentations made, since people already supportive of the clientele do not generally need as much (if any) sophisticated analysis, well-reasoned arguments, or comprehensive reviews of previous research on the clientele affected by the policy as other kinds of audiences may. Instead, they need to be aroused, mobilized, and drawn into the debate or political process which is dealing with issues affecting this clientele group.

The primary audience of the *technician,* the second role type, would be his/her peers. Peers in this discussion refer to other advice givers who claim expertise in the same policy area. Therefore, peers might be: fellow economists, political scientists, sociologists, policy analysts, planners, evaluators, agency workers, agency directors, and so on, involved in the same area or any other individuals perceived by the technician to be an expert advice giver. The importance of peers is that the technician's *primary audience* may not be the clientele affected by policy, the organization implementing the policy, or even the decision makers formulating the policy, but rather people who perceive of themselves as expert advice givers. The real audience of many economists is really other economists. The real audience of many policy analysts is other policy analysts. And the real audience of agency workers is other agency workers. In preparing written documents and making oral presentations, the technician is acutely aware of the standards and norms of his/her peers, and thus technicians orient their work toward these standards and norms. If sophisticated methodology, a certain theory, a particular analytical technique, and a set of ethical or normative values are predominant within this peer group, then the technician is obliged to deal with these norms in their work. Often people *outside* of this peer system read a policy document or hear a presentation and react by saying it is too jargonized, too theoretical, unfeasible, basically irrelevant to the real world or the like. I suspect that this reaction is based fundamentally on the fact that advice givers who perceive of themselves as technicians are not trying very hard to consciously address potential audiences that are outside of their perceived peers.

This sets up a dynamic of inbreeding, isolation, and insulation which often means advice seekers have little use for technicians unless these technicians can translate their work in a way that makes it understandable and clear to the decision maker. The secondary audiences of the technician are the decision makers who will debate and decide on policy and the organizational and institutional leadership directly responsible for developing and implementing policy in this area. It is worth emphasizing again that the primary audience of the technician is considerably different from that of the dramatist.

The third role type is that of the *pragmatist*. The primary audience of the pragmatist would be the organizational and institutional leadership directly responsible for developing and implementing policy in a particular area. The pragmatist wants something to get done, above all. What will go and what is feasible are critical. Organizational and institutional leaders usually behave in a way that suggests that their basic responsibility is maintenance of policy and programs in an area and, therefore, feasible, incremental changes or recommendations are desired. The pragmatist is oriented toward fulfilling the expectations of these kinds of "advice seekers." As such, pragmatists focus their work on providing clear, dejargonized, feasible, and the implementable advice and recommendations. They are less interested in the arousal or mobilization of audiences or appealing to professional norms or standards — rather they direct their attention to the institutional or organizational leadership directly responsible for this policy area.

The pragmatists' secondary audiences are those decision makers generally who debate and decide on policy in this area and clientele or interest groups representing them that are directly affected by policy in this area. The appeal would be to getting something done, moving the field ahead, and modifying policy even though it would only be an incremental improvement.

In summary, the three political role types distinguish between different personal role expectations on the part of advice givers. *Dramatists seek to activate, arouse, and ultimately mobilize audiences already supporting a particular policy perspective or position. Technicians are oriented toward their peers as they perceive them and accordingly they seek to be consistent with peer norms and standards. Finally, pragmatists are seeking to show leaders how to keep the policy area moving ahead, it is hoped through incremental improvement.*

STOP AND THINK

How many dramatists, technicians, and pragmatists do you know? What things about each of these role types frustrate you? What things about these role types do you agree with? How well do you interact with each role type?

If relevant audiences can be distinguished to a certain degree, then the kinds of advice they want, and need, can be distinguished as well. Table 2 highlights some ideas about the kinds of advice certain audiences seek. While the kinds of advice are broad, they do help one to see that not every audience necessarily wants and needs the same

TABLE 2   Audiences and Kinds of Advice Sought

Audience	Kinds of Advice Sought		
	Nature	*Specificity*	*Balance*
Clientele Directly Affected	Appeal to shared values	Very specific and tangible	One sided and explicit
Interest Groups Representing Clientele	Appeal to shared values	Very specific and tangible	One sided and explicit
Organizations and Leaders Directly Responsible for Clientele	Reasonableness and completeness of argument	Very specific and tangible	Only feasible options or alternatives
Peers or Experts	Supportable by data, research, and logic	Neutral, ambiguous, or very broad	As many sides as possible, comprehensive alternatives
Predisposed Decision Makers	Appeal to shared values	Very specific and tangible	One sided and explicit
Decision Makers Generally	All of above	All of above	All of above

kinds of advice. Given the previous discussion on roles and audiences, it is hypothesized that affected clientele, clientele interest groups, and predisposed decision makers do not really need a lot of comprehensive information, analyses, or carefully reasoned arguments; but rather they need advice about how to mobilize, arouse, reinforce, and activate people and organizations in order to support, in a political sense, the movement in a certain policy direction.

If these are the major things they need advice about, then advice givers should appeal to shared values, be very specific and clear about their policy recommendations, and emphasize explicitly how the interests of the clientele can be advanced. This may seem like a harsh or narrow perspective on advice, yet advice seekers who are largely already committed to certain policy objectives want to know which values to appeal to and which recommendations (specifically) will enhance the interests of their clientele the most. Much advice is needed in these areas and certainly the advice givers oriented toward these audiences ought to consider whether they are, in fact, giving these kinds of advice. The personal role expectation of the dramatist best characterizes advice givers who can fulfill the expectations of these audiences.

In contrast, peers or experts are more interested in the "objectivity" of the advice giver. This usually translates into whether the advice is supported by evidence that has been collected, analyzed, and interpreted according to professional standards and norms. Additionally, is there a comprehensive and exhaustive set of alternatives or options for dealing with the policy problem arrayed for consideration? And finally, does the advice giver remain neutral in terms of recommendations, thus leaving the advice seeker with the job of deciding which option is more desirable?

The notion of "objectivity" is premised on the very conventional and traditional view that analysis should be neutral as to values, with the implication that value neutrality corresponds closely with the meaning of science and the scientific method. This, of course, does not mean that values are not present in this kind of advice giving, but only that they are not explicit or conscious and, more important, that the advice givers here want to create the impression of "objectivity" which is reinforced by minimizing the role of explicit values. The personal role expectation of the *technicians* best characterizes advice givers who can fulfill the expectations of this kind of audience.

Organizations and their leaders who are directly responsible for developing or implementing policy in a particular area are primarily concerned with advice that will allow them to maintain the current or existing base of policy for a particular clientele. At the same time they attempt to move in a positive, but feasible direction. While they may personally prefer a radical shift in policy, they see their main role as that of maintaining what currently exists while moving ahead in a positive direction. This usually is interpreted as advice that will enhance incremental change. Therefore, advice givers who focus only on feasible alternatives, develop complete rationals (whether quantitative or qualitative) for these alternatives, and make recommendations very specific are in demand by these kinds of advice seekers. The personal role expectations of this kind of audience.

The last audience in Table 2 are the "decision makers." From one perspective, they are the hardest audience to deal with. Decision makers who are predisposed toward certain policy positions and decision makers holding specific institutional or organizational leadership positions have already been discussed. However, decision makers who have no preexisting policy position or stance may need all the kinds of advice illustrated in Table 2. Perhaps this means that such things as personality, decision-making style, previous professional experience, educational background, and so on may explain the kinds of advice needed by these decision makers.

Having explored some possible relationships between the three roles and audiences and kinds of advice, another important dimension of this discussion is the advice giver's choice of the different modes of participation. Important modes of participation to consider are the

TABLE 3   Roles and Modes of Participation

	Modes of Participation		
Roles	*Scope of Involvement*[1]	*Base of Operation*[2]	*Intent or Goals*[3]
Dramatist	All except Development and Structuring of Alternatives	External and Internal	Direct impact Short term impact Explicit goals/values
Technician	Problem Specification Development & Structuring of Alternatives Evaluation, Assessment, Refurbishment	Internal and External	Indirect impact Long term impact Implicit goals & value
Pragmatist	All stages in process	Internal	Direct & indirect impact Short term impact Explicit/implicit goals and values

NOTES: 1. Scope of Involvement:

   Problem Specification; Development and Structuring of Alternatives; Ratification and Acceptance; Implementation; and Evaluation, Assessment, and Refurbishment.

2. Base of Operation:

   Internal -   Executive departments, legislative staff, intra-agency or departmental task forces, government corporations or quasi-governmental units;

   External -   interest groups, consulting firms, institutes or think tanks, academia, special commissions, etc.

3. Intent or Goals:

   Direct or indirect impact
   Short or long term impact
   Explicit or implicit goal/values

scope of involvement, the base of operation, and the intent or goals of the advice givers. Table 3 is suggestive of what these expectations might be in a general way.

A conventional view of the problem-solving process suggests a number of phases: Problem Specification; Development and Structuring of Alternatives; Ratification and Acceptance; Implementation; and Evaluation, Assessment, and Refurbishment. All of these phases taken together are referred to as the policy machinery used to generate and ultimately implement policy objectives. However, the question is whether the personal role expectations of the dramatists, technicians, and pragmatists differ as to what their scope of involvement in the policy machinery should be. Table 3 offers some interpretations of these differences.

The pragmatist is primarily concerned with promoting and securing incremental change, so it seems reasonable to think that attention (even if modest) should be paid to all phases of the process, since neglect of any major phase may mean policy failure or stalemate. On the other hand, dramatists are equally interested in positive change and policy success for their clientele, so they should give attention for the same reasons to all phases — except possibly the development and structuring of alternatives. This is excluded because the dramatist's position or alternative is generally developed early and other options are rarely examined seriously, unless it is absolutely necessary from a political standpoint during the ratification phase. The tendency is for dramatists to make their alternative known and demand that others accommodate their alternatives to this one.

Finally, the technician, armed with the scientific method and the techniques associated with it, eschews phases that involve bargaining, compromising, exerting influence, accommodation or trade-offs, implementation or administration, and so on and emphasizes phases that maximize the utility of data collection, data analysis, and data interpretation. Thus, the phases of problem specification, alternative generation, and evaluation are the best candidates for those oriented to the scientific method.

When looking at the range of organizational settings in which advice givers may operate, the pragmatist should seek a base of operation that is both internal to the formal governmental decision-making process as well as close to the authoritative decision makers themselves. As illustrated in Table 3, pragmatists should gravitate, therefore, to executive departments, Congresspeople and committees, important task forces or commissions, and so on and *that the closer the pragmatist is to the top of the organization or to authoritative decision makers, the better* (in terms of fulfilling intended role expectations).

While dramatists might, and occasionally do, infiltrate the internal and formal decision-making process, their influence is largely determined by their ability to generate political support on the outside (external) and bring it to bear on the internal processes. It is hard to say numerically whether true dramatists are more likely to be employed externally or internally, though I suspect dramatists on the inside over time become co-opted by the agency or unit they work for. Since it is at least questionable, the base of operation is indicated as both internal and external; but there should be a distinct preference for an external base of operation since dramatists find it hard to pursue their objectives on the inside.

While there has been a proliferation of external organizations dealing with policy, there are a significant number of technicians on the inside. The preferred base of operation for the technicians should be internal, though there are enough on the outside to indicate that both must be discussed. The preference for an internal base of operation for the technician is based on the reasoning that: getting access to data is easier on the inside; and communicating with a network of technicians in a particular policy area is easier to accomplish on the inside because of proximity. All of this argues that the preferred base should be internal.

Given the previous discussion of roles, it is reasonable to posit that dramatists are more likely to want to have a direct, explicit, and short-run impact on policy, while technicians are more likely to want to have an implicit and indirect impact on policy in the short run; and to do this he or she must seek directly or indirectly and explicitly or implicitly to accomplish this short-term, incremental goal. In this context, the pragmatist and dramatist may win most of the battles but the technician may win the war. Or, depending upon your perspective, it may be the reverse.

Even if the advice giver has clearly pinpointed his or her intended audience, clarified the kinds of advice different audiences seek, explored and diagnosed the most appropriate mode of participation that can be pursued, there is still a question of whether the advice giver has a sufficiently demonstrated range of knowledge to be judged competent. Dramatists have mastered certain combinations of knowledge, technicians other combinations, and pragmatists still other combinations. There are many ways to categorize the knowledge or skill area of advice givers. Consistent with the ideas presented so far, knowledge is separated into three areas: policy nomenclature and policy history; policy machinery and strategy; and research, analysis, and written documentation.

Knowledge about policy nomenclature; policy history; research, analysis, and written documentation; and the ability to perform tasks associated with this kind of knowledge are basically substantive in nature. Acquisition of these kinds of substantive knowledge requires a great deal of formal training and/or practical experience. This knowledge is less interpersonal and social and is more analytical in nature.

Alternatively, knowledge about policy machinery and strategy and the ability to perform tasks associated with this knowledge are more social and interactive in nature in that they depend heavily on the understanding of such things as personality, style, and successful interpersonal communication. *Good advice would be to acquire and*

TABLE 4   Role and Types of Knowledge

	Types of Knowledge		
ROLE	*Policy nomenclature (concepts, frameworks, perspectives, etc.) and policy history*	*Policy machinery and strategy*	*Research, analysis, and written documentation*
Dramatist	Limited amount generally, but expert when relating to their target group and programs affecting group	A great deal of expertise	Extremely limited
Technician	Expert on policy nomenclature, but moderate on policy history	Limited expertise in machinery, almost nothing on strategy	Expert
Pragmatist	A great deal about both nomenclature and history	Expert in all phases	Limited and used only to legitimize position

master knowledge that can be categorized as both analytical and social or interactive. Yet as Table 4 suggests, the *pragmatist* is most proficient in the understanding and use of policy machinery and strategy, reasonably proficient in policy nomenclature and history, and weakest in research, analysis, and written documentation.

In contrast, the *technician* is strongest in research and such, reasonably strong in policy nomenclature and policy history, and weakest in policy machinery and strategy. Finally, the *dramatist* is similar to the pragmatist in combinations of knowledge except that dramatists are far more specialized in terms of nomenclature and history as it relates directly to their clientele groups than is the pragmatist. The pragmatist usually has a broader understanding and range of experiences than the dramatist.

One generalization that can be made from this discussion is that pragmatists and dramatists are more similar than dissimilar, and technicians are different from both of them because their knowledge is so specialized. Another generalization is that pragmatists and dramatists, by necessity, have extraordinary social and interactive skills and moderate amounts of analytical skills, but technicians have almost the reverse combination — they are strong analytically and weak in interactive skills. Finally, formal academic and disciplinary training for practitioners is largely one emphasizing analytical skills. This means, as a generalization, that interactive skills are largely inherited or acquired (if at all) indirectly through various socialization experiences.

Table 5 summarizes the discussion. Three role types have been developed and connected to the intended targets of advice, the kinds of advice given, the modes of participation pursued, and the combinations of knowledge sought. The role types are analytical constructs, and it would be fair to argue that an individual advice giver may wear many different hats and, in fact, they may combine audiences, kinds of advice, modes of participation, and expert knowledge in many different ways. While advice givers may combine these facets of advice in different ways, these analytical constructs emphasize in each case the primary or central motivating behavior of the advice giver. On balance, it is reasonable to argue that advice givers play a *predominant* role most of the time, even if they occasionally wear a different hat. Concomitantly, as they play this predominant role, they develop a common set of practices for giving advice. Again, this is not to say that they do not stray from this predominant role or common set

TABLE 5   Summary of Relationship Between Roles and Audiences, Kinds of Advice, Modes of Participation, and Types of Knowledge

Roles	Primary Audience	Kinds of Advice	Dominant Modes of Participation	Expert Knowledge
Dramatist	Clientele Clientele groups Predisposed decision makers	Appeal to values Specific & tangible recommendations One sided	Most phases of process Preference for external base of operation Direct/short term	Policy machinery and strategy (Both interactive and analytical)
Technician	Peers	Data analysis and logic Neutral advice Comprehensive alternatives	Limited phases of process Preference for internal base of operation Indirect/long term	Research, analysis and written documentation (analytical)
Pragmatist	Organizational and Institutionalized leadership	Reasonableness and completeness of argument Specific recommendations Feasible alternatives only	All phases of process Internal base of operation Direct & indirect/short term	Policy machinery and strategy (Both interactive and analytical)

of advice-giving practices occasionally, but only that the role constructs introduced here explain in a behavioral sense the typical role patterns in the policy world.

In conclusion, political advisors must be far more sensitive to the needs of different audiences. They must be willing to change the kind of advice given so that it more clearly meets the needs of the intended audience. Otherwise, they will be less successful in having their advice followed by a broader set of audiences. Second, and attendant to the first point, advisors seeking to accommodate wider ranges of audiences must acquire a more balanced set of skills (knowledge) if they are to be successful. Third, if advice givers seek to influence different phases of the policy process, then they must acquire the knowledge necessary to do so or they will be confined to only a very narrow phase of the policy formulation and implementation process which means diminished amounts of influence over the final product. Fourth, advice givers need to consider carefully their base of operation and whether the vantage point provided by that base maximizes their opportunity to provide useful advice.

Finally, political advisors over time acquire a great deal of knowledge through experience opposed to formal training, yet fundamentally I would argue that the personal role expectation of the advisor is what is important since this will dictate more than anything else what they do when they organize and present their work to others. And ultimately it depends on who one is trying to give advice to and can it be done more effectively or competently. *Effectiveness is enhanced by being clear about audiences, being careful to tailor advice so that it meets the needs of the intended audience, being realistic about what modes of participation can be pursued in order to connect one's advice with the intended audience, and being aggressive in the acquisition of knowledge necessary to fulfill the role most desired by the individual political advisor.*

The appropriate role should be closely linked with the decision-making styles and oreintations of key actors. Table 6 connects the discussion so far. It indicates a summary of the major role types, the decision-making audiences they primarily appeal to, and the other attributes each role type has.

EXERCISE

Have each participant profile three different actors that they are familiar with, assess their decision-making style, establish their information needs,

TABLE 6 Roles, Skills, Competencies and Decision-making Audiences

Policy Roles	Summary of Major Skills, Competencies and Decision-Making Audiences
Dramatist	*Best able to relate to emotional/ideological decision-making styles.* Skilled at preparing "Quick & Dirty" memos and Think Pieces Designs recommendations for short term and instrumental use Knowledgeable in almost all phases of the policy process Handles highly consensual decision making situations very well, able to motivate and raise consciousness
Technician	*Best able to relate to rationalist/deliberative decision-making styles.* Skilled at preparing comprehensive analyses and doing or interpreting basic research Able to influence conceptual and long-term view of problem Knowledgeable in selected phases of the policy process (problem specification, alternative generation, evaluation) Handles decision-making situations where there are not clear preferences present very well
Pragmatist	*Best able to relate to pragmatic/incremental decision-making styles.* Skilled at preparing policy options memorandum, "Quick & Dirty" and Think Pieces Designs recommendations for short-term and instrumental use Knowledgeable in all phases of the policy process Handles highly conflictual decision-making situations very well, resolves conflict through bargaining

and choose a role that should be used when they interact with these actors. The group leader should make sure that each participant profiles these actors carefully in light of the discussion in this chapter and also that the participant honestly assesses what roles should be played as a result of doing the profiles accurately. Some participants will indicate that in the past they have played the wrong role given this kind of analysis. That means the exercise is working since they will now modify their role to reflect the analysis of decision makers' needs. Finally, ask participants to select one decision maker they have had particular trouble with in the past.

Ask them to profile this person, select a role, and present their findings to the full group. The full group should then critique (in a helpful way) each participant presentation. In very large groups, participants could merely present this to the person sitting closest to them. However, when time permits, these presentations and the feedback received can be most helpful to individual participants. A recent application of this exercise revealed the following decision-making styles as they applied to people who participants had interacted with. The participants then examined their respective roles when they dealt with each person.

SAMPLE

Pragmatic	Rational Deliberative	Emotional Ideological
Board President	Office of Management and Budget	Board President
County Department of Social Services	Board Secretary	
Board Chairman	Fiscal Officer	Finance Committee Chairperson
Executive Director	Executive Director, Justice Commission	Mayor
Regional Program Director	Chairman, Advisory Group	Advisory Committee
Director of State Office	Director of State Human Service Agency	
Mayor	Archbishop	Agency Director
Regional Program Director	County Supervisor	Legislator
Legislative Staff	Board Member	Coordinator in program
County Supervisor	Director of Zoning	Judge
County Probate Judge		Program Manager
Director of Community-Based Program		Board Chairman

NOTE

1. In this context, the successful political advocate is being referred to as an "advice giver" since this is consistent with the function being performed.

REFERENCES

ABERBACH, J. (1976) "Clashing beliefs within the executive branch." American Political Science Review 456-468.

DERTHICK, M. (1975) Uncontrollable Spending for Social Services Grants. Washington, DC: Brookings Institution.

HECLO, H. (1977) A Government of Strangers. Washington, DC: Brookings Institution.

PRESSMAN, J. and A. WILDAVSKY (1973) Implementation. Berkeley: University of California Press.

STEINER, G. Y. (1976) The Children's Cause. Washington, DC: Brookings Institution.

TROPMAN, J., et al. (1976) Strategic Perspectives on Social Policy. Elmsford, NY: Pergamon.

VAN METER, D. (1975) "The policy implementation process." Administration and Society 7: 445-488.

WEISS, C. (1977) Using Social Research in Public Policy Making. Lexington, MA: D. C, Heath.

Chapter 6

COALITION BUILDING

BACKGROUND AND ASSUMPTIONS

One of the most difficult tasks of the political advocate is to organize enough political support to achieve policy success. The political advocate may be a member of an existing organization which has limited and narrow purposes, but he or she may be called upon to mobilize a number of organizations including his or her own. These organizations have to be put together in a way so that the political base is capable of determining and shaping the policy outcomes. *The major and primary purpose of a coalition is political – that is, the achievement of policy objectives in the political process.* While the coalition is functioning, it may serve secondary purposes as well, like providing social experiences for its members, disseminating information in an educational way to its members, and allowing people in the coalition to change jobs and responsibilities. But the political purpose of the coalition is paramount. *The formation of a successful coalition is derived from a comprehensive understanding of the dynamics of coalition formation.* Much is learned through experience, but there are some key concepts and attributes which can be helpful in providing a useful perspective for figuring out the steps necessary to build successful coalitions.

CONCEPTS AND ILLUSTRATIONS

Table 7 summarizes the major types and kinds of coalitions found in the American political process. As you move down the table from ad hoc to permanent coalitions, the characteristics of each type of coalition are portrayed. Each column, therefore, represents a critical aspect of coalition formation. Reading down the table illustrates the dynamics of coalition formation.

Short-term coalitions which go out of existence after a single issue is raised and resolved are less desirable than those organized around an ideology, because the former must start from the beginning (or over) each time, while the latter merely draws upon an existing and permanent base. After a time, political advocates expend their personal resources because it is very time consuming and frustrating to build ad hoc and shoestring coalitions over and over again, *de novo.* On the other hand, federated, integrated, and permanent coalitions are easier to mobilize, and they can be put together more quickly with less effort.

STOP AND THINK

How many of these different kinds of coalitions have you either observed or been part of? Did these coalitions have other important characteristics not indicated in Table 7?

The challenge for any coalition is to take a single issue and organize around it, move on to another issue and do the same, and keep doing this successfully until there is a stable cadre of leaders, organizations, and resources available for mobilization regardless of the specific issue. Over time, coalitions begin to rely on a combination of both charismatic and pragmatic leadership. Finally, the value or ideological base of coalitions tends to move from looseness and diversity toward narrowness and consistency.

All of this argues that some coalitions can move through the various phases toward permanency, while other remain at one phase or in some cases even move backward. The obvious question is what determines movement through these various phases? Does leadership come first? Then resource acquisition? Then vertical organiza-

TABLE 7   Types of Coalitions

Name	Basis for Coalition	Stability	Major Resources	Group Activity	When to Use	Value or Ideo-logical Base	Leadership Style	Illustrations
Ad hoc	Organized around a single issue, event or person	Unstable, short run, goes out of existence after issue dealt with	Symbolic, coercive	Dramatic and time limited, coordin-ation is ad hoc	Timely issue, limited resources	Loose and varied	Charismatic & personality oriented	Social Svs. Groups Youth Groups Rural Poor Indian Groups
Shoe string	Organized around a single issue, event or person	Unstable, stays together 6 mos. to 2 yrs., searches for new issue, event, or person	Symbolic, coercive	Loose coalition of small no. of groups, emerging leadership, but no staff	Timely issue, limited resources, li-mited volunteers & leaders	Loose and varied	Charismatic & personality oriented Indian Groups	Social Svs. Groups Youth Groups Rural Poor
Federated	Organized around a number of issues which may be in conflict	Stable, but hard to mobil-ize because issue must be appealing	Symbolic, limited, utilitarian	Loose coalition of large no. of groups, rotating leadership some staff	Good working relations with groups of some-what different interests	Core ideology but tolerates some dissenting ideologies	Pragmatic who keeps loose coalition together	Child Welfare Grps. Mental Health Grps. Women's Rights Grps. Black Groups
Inte-grated	Organized around a series of is-sues which are interrelated & which leader-ship agrees on	Stable, easy to mobilize because issues are rele-vant to groups	All	Tight coalition of groups, verti-cal organizational network, stable leadership, per-manent staff, lobbying office	Many resources, important issue has been surfaced	Narrow ideological base	Pragmatic in terms of mobilizing resources	Ecology Groups Elderly Groups Housing Groups Airlines Farm Groups
Perma-nent	Organized around an ideology, permanent lea-dership cadre, & historical events & successes	Stable, easy to mobilize be-cause seen as ideology	All	All of the above, plus the coalition has many of its mem-bers in decision making positions	All the time, if it exists	Very narrow and doctrinaire ideological base	Pragmatic and charismatic	Anti-War Groups Pro-Israel Aid Groups Oil/Petroleum Groups Hospital Groups Pro-Minimum Wage Groups

69

tion networks? With so many different kinds of coalitions, it is almost impossible to make confident generalizations. Nevertheless, experience and some of the research cited at the end of the chapter suggest that: the availability of resources; the kins, quality, and stability of leadership available; and the clarity and political attractiveness of the ideological base to the larger public are the most important.

The coalition-building game used as an exercise in this chapter, if played a number of times and observed carefully, will reveal all of the dynamics presented in Table 7. Coalitions are also contingent on their external environment and often uncontrollable historical events provide the beginning for what turns out to be a permanent coalition a few years later. The Great Depression was the impetus for the labor coalition; the Arab embargo for the oil coalition; and the total failure of the military in Vietnam for the antiwar coalition. Understanding the field of coalition building is a real challenge since most people have little historical perspective on the incremental steps that took place with some of the more successful and permanent coalitions. But the way to proceed is to examine the attributes (listed in Table 7), apply them to successful and unsuccessful coalitions you are familiar with, and then determine whether and in which sequence these attributes were present.

Next, pick a political area you are interested in and outline a series of steps that you would follow to move from one type of coalition to another. The concepts in Table 7 should help you to perform this kind of analysis; the analysis, however, may determine that resources are critical but not indicate how to acquire them. It may indicate that a more pragmatic leadership style is demanded but not how to attract such leadership to the coalition. The challenge to the political advocate is to analyze the dynamics, decide on priorities among the attributes that should be developed, and develop the action steps to move from one type of coalition to another. It is important to clarify the attributes and dynamics of coalitions. The action steps necessary to move toward more permanency should be debated and weighed by the members of the coalition. This presentation provides a framework (Table 7) that allows these members to assess where they are going and what is required to go further.

EXERCISE

After reading this chapter, perhaps more than once, and reviewing Table 7 carefully, you are ready to apply the concepts by playing the simulation

SILOS. Some preliminary things should be considered before playing the game. They are:

(1) You need at least 12 people to play; you can add more roles, following the format used with the roles below, but no more than 25 people is recommended.

(2) You need a game operator and at least two observers. The operator gives out chips, orients group to game, and leads discussion afterward. The observers watch the game and make generalizations during the discussion period about the dynamics of coalition formation.

(3) You need six different color poker chips. White chips with orange, purple, black, and so on stickers will serve purpose because most stores have only three colors of chips. Different colored squares of paper can be substituted for the chips.

(4) Allow two hours for the game: 10 to 15 minutes of orientation, one hour to play the game and the rest of the time to discuss or debrief. Roles should be handed out ahead of time so people can familiarize themselves with their respective roles (perhaps the night before or a few hours before).

(5) You need a large room with comfortable chairs and couches so people can move around freely.

OBJECT OF GAME

The object is to form a coalition of actors, draft a proposal for the state Title XX agency, assemble the resources (chips) of the actors, and get the proposal funded. Only one proposal can be funded in the game but the funding agency may review as many proposals as it receives. An acceptable proposal must follow "Form X" and include the resources (chips) of the coalition. If the proposal is turned down, the chips are returned to various actors and the process starts over. Only *one* proposal can be funded during the game.

RULES OF THE GAME[1]

(1) The funding agency (state Title XX agency) can fund only one proposal during the game, and it can do so at any time.

(2) Funding agency (consisting of three people) must take first 10 minutes of game to establish priorities for funding and the procedure they will use to review proposals when they come in. These *priorities* and *procedures* should be written down and available to actors in the game. *This must be done in first 10 minutes by funding agency.* A vote of two

of the three members of the funding agency is necessary for a proposal to be approved.

(3)   First 10 minutes for funding agency to meet (separately) while other actors familiarize themselves with other actors in game. Roles should be done up on index cards and pinned to the shirt or blouse of each player so they can walk around and read each other's tag. Tags remain on for the rest of the game.

(4)   Form "X" is necessary before funding agency will consider proposal (sample included below). Resources or chips must be submitted along with proposal.

(5)   If proposal is not funded, chips are returned to respective actors.

(6)   Funding agency must spend its money by end of game.

(7)   Funding agency can accept any proposal as long as it meets one of the following goals.

   (a)   Enhances the summer job opportunities for youth living in the inner city and coming from low-income families.

   (b)   Coordinates and increases the ability of the community service organizations to serve the short-term crisis needs of distressed youth in the community.

   (c)   Decreases the incidence of youth prostitution in the community.

"Form X"

1. Goals of Program _____

2. Organization or Delivery Design _____

3. Sponsorship for program _____

4. Record of people submitting proposal (their experience) _____

_____

5. Governance of Program _____

6. Resources (include chips)
   Money
   Energy
   Facilities
   Political legitimacy
   Expertise/knowledge
   Political mobilization

(Form should be only one page. Players should briefly fill out each part of form based on the coalition's agreement.)

Resources (Chips)

MONEY (red)	= tangible resources
ENERGY (blue)	= volunteers, time, willingness to give free time
FACILITIES (white)	= offices, equipment, cars, and so on
POLITICAL LEGITIMACY (yellow)	= political support and popularity in community
EXPERTISE/ KNOWLEDGE (orange)	= legal, financial, organizational, and so on
POLITICAL MOBILIZATION (green)	= ability to mobilize members of their organizations for political purposes.

Each player is given the designated amounts of chips (listed at end of role section). Some players have more of some kinds of resources than others. Players should figure this out as game goes on. Hand out chips at beginning of game. The idea is to allow coalitions to form which have different combinations of resources. The funding agency should certainly take these resources into account when it is making its decision. For example, you would not want to fund a proposal without any or with few facilities available to implement a program or correspondingly one that did not have access to expertise/knowledge.

Community Setting

Alcoa is a diverse, urbanized, and industrialized county in a midwestern state. In the last 10 years, the county has experienced serious economic and social problems. The unemployment rate fluctuates between 9% and 14%, depending on the status of the steel industry, the main employer. Crime rates, divorce rates, child abuse and neglect cases, spouse abuse cases, and so on all increase and decrease with the unemployment rate. One-third of the county is rural, small town, and very conservative on taxes, budget, and policy issues (i.e., they are generally opposed to funding social service type programs). Approximately a third of the county is urban and blue-collar with high percentages of minority groups. Their unemployment rate is high and the need for social service programs is greatest. They are liberal on programs targeted to their area but very conservative on tax and budget issues. The other third of the county is urban but the residents are white middle to upper class. They are mixed toward the need for social service programs but they can be convinced. However, they are very conservative on tax and budget issues.

Community Influential
BANK PRESIDENT

A. *Background*

Joseph Phillips

52 years old

Community leader

Well-known and noted for fairness

Always interested in how issues will affect economic development in the city

Solid family man

Raises basset hounds

Republican

B. Conservative

C. Pragmatist

D. Friends with Judge and Ester Weatherbee

CHIEF OF POLICE

A. *Background*

Chester Marcol

52 years old

White

Native of community

BA in Criminology

Democrat

Well liked by politicians

Two teen-aged children

Wife is paraprofessional in community
mental health system

B. Liberal

C. Pragmatist

D. Long-time association and friendship
with bank president and judge

EXECUTIVE DIRECTOR
— Urban League

A. *Background*

John Johnson

Black

30 years old

M.S.W.

Upwardly mobile

Urban League 5 years

Former H.S. dropout

Completed undergrad degree while
working full time

B. Liberal

C. Pragmatist

D. Recently took class with Bonnie Radine,
Ph. D.

Working relationship with Arturo Rangel

EXECUTIVE DIRECTOR
— Community Mental Health

A. *Background*
   Fred Sommers
   Calm, cool, collected
   41 years old
   Background in Business Management
   Former comptroller for CMH agency
   Single
   Low Key

B. Conservative

C. Technician

D. Has a Board of Directors that could
      involve some of the other actors in
      this game

   Has had some conflicts in past with
      liberals

PRESIDENT
— League of Women Voters

A. *Background*

   Agnes Chapman

   MA, 49 years old

   Husband is successful stockbroker

   Admirer of Walter Cronkite and John Anderson

   A lot of time on hands

   Volunteers for everything

   Uses time wisely

   3 teen-aged children — ACTING OUT

B. Liberal

C. Technician

D. Gets salary w/League of Women Voters

   Friends with Judge, Police Chief, Mental Health and School

FUNDING AGENCY
— Dept. of Human Resources

A. *Background*

Lillian White

32 years old

Director of local abortion clinic

Chairwoman of the State Committee on Abortion Rights

Adamant about the rights of all women

Opinionated, dramatic, competitive

Has been known to engage in lengthy shouting debates

Got appointed to funding agency to pacify women's movement

B. Radical

C. Emotional/Ideological

D. No real alignments

PROBATE JUDGE

A. *Background*

    Harry F. White

    55 years old

    Judge for 25 years

    Raised in foster home — not very warm parents, worked hard for everything he ever got

    Earned way through law school

    Married to daughter of construction worker

    One child currently doctor went to school with Emily's daughter

B. Conservative

C. Emotional/Ideological

D. Allies — Fred Phillips, Bank President; Grayburn Rooster, conservative ally; Police Chief

COMMUNITY LIAISON
— for the School District

A. *Background*
   Ester Schwartz
   42 years old
   MA in counseling
   Knows county well
   Family oriented
   20 years in school system
   Grew up in small town outside of Boston

B. Conservative

C. Technician

D. Aloof, no friends

FUNDING AGENCY
— Dept. of Human Resources

A. *Background*

Grayburn Rooster

57 years old

Former state legislator

Republican

Fiscal conservative

Anti-service programs

Wants to ignore urban part of county

Has 4 daughters; one granddaughter who
    is handicapped

Conservative on women's role in society

Law and order type

B. Conservative

C. Pragmatist

D. Friends with judge

COUNTY BOARD OF SUPERVISORS

A. *Background*

Ester Walker

28 years old

White

Radical, elected from radical student political base which has vanished

Organizer of food co-op in inner city

Adamant about women's rights and child abuse

Opinionated, dramatic, dogmatic

Been pretty much of a loner, no history with other actors

B. Radical

C. Emotional/Ideological

D. No friends

PROJECT DIRECTOR
— Legal Advocacy Clinic for Youth

A. *Background*

Arturo Rangel, lawyer

35 years old

Bright, ambitious, 3 degrees

Democratic

Charismatic leader in Hispanic community

Pet interest in migrant youth

Committed to inner city and its problems

Excellent public speaker

B. Liberal

C. Emotional/Ideological

D. Working relationship with John Johnson

Was volunteer attorney for ad hoc committee which was successful in bringing a Job Corps Center to the county 6 years ago

FUNDING AGENCY
— Dept. of Human Resources

A. *Background*

Bonnie Radine, Ph. D.

39 years old

Professor of the School of Social Work

Good analytical mind, needs to be convinced

Considerable interest in planning and collaborative efforts

Recently has experienced self-doubt about her career and personal life

Divorced

B. Liberal

C. Technician

D. John Johnson, former classmate

Natural friend of Ester Schwartz

COMMUNITY INFLUENTIAL
— President of the Art Society

A. *Background*

Emily Weatherbee

53 years old

Daughter of "old money" family

Very active in a variety of liberal,
social causes since the 1960s,
long association with other liberals
including League of Women Voters.

29-year-old daughter, went to school
with son of Probate Judge,
Harry White.

B. Liberal

C. Pragmatist

D. Has been in contact over the years with
almost all the other actors

Socialite

DIRECTOR OF THE BUDGET
— for the City

A. *Background*

    Alan M. Phister

    31 years old

    BA in accounting

    Precise, demanding

    Married, no children

    Requires extensive justification for everything

    Fanatic professional football fan

    Vietnam vet

    Constant pressure from city manager to keep budget in line

B. Conservative

C. Technician

D. Few friends except Fred Sommers

Distribution of Chips

Actor	red	blue	white	yellow	orange	green
			Number of Chips			
Bank President	15	7	0	9	15	3
Chief of Police	0	4	0	4	0	0
Executive Director (Urban League)	10	10	10	4	0	3
Executive Director (Community Mental Health)	0	7	16	0	4	0
President of League of Women Voters	15	15	0	9	0	6
*Department of Human Resources	0	0	0	0	0	0
Probate Judge	5	0	0	4	0	3
Community Liaison	0	7	10	0	3	0
Member County Board of Supervisors	0	0	0	0	0	10
Project Director	10	10	10	1	3	0
President of Art Society	15	15	0	9	0	0
Director of Budget	5	0	0	0	15	0
TOTALS	75	75	46	40	40	25

*There are three roles designated as Department of Human Resources. These roles are within the funding agency. They do not need chips because they are not involved in coalition building but only making the decision on the proposals.

Debriefing (About ½ Hour)

Game Operator and observers lead discussion, but everyone should participate. Some areas to cover are:

(1) who played leadership roles

(2) problems and successes in forming coalitions

(3) dynamics of funding agency

(4) how much thought went into proposal

(5) which people got together and why

(6) comparison in terms of size, ideology, resources of the different coalitions formed

(7) appeal used by different coalitions.

NOTE

1. This game uses goals from the youth area. You can easily change these goals to reflect ones that are found in areas like child welfare, aging, spouse abuse, handicapped, and so on. The only thing that would be necessary to adapt this game to areas representing other disadvantaged groups would be to modify some of the background information under each role. The changes in background information should be made to reflect the kinds of people who normally get involved in the area you choose to play the game in. Therefore, this is a *general* game aimed at showing the dynamics of coalition formation at the community level. It is only necessary to change the goals of the funding agency and modify somewhat the background information under each role to make the game applicable to other areas.

REFERENCES

DEXTER, A. (1969) How Organizations Are Represented in Washington. (Indianapolis: Bobbs-Merrill.
LAUFFER. A. (1973) The Aim of the Game. New York: Gamed Simulations, Inc.
OLSON, M. (1968) The Logic of Collective Action. New York: Schocken Books.
PATTI, R. (1975) "Legislative advocacy: One path to social change." Social Work 20: 108-114.
REDMAN, E. (1974) The Dance of Legislation. New York: Simon and Schuster.
ROSS, R. (1970) "Relations among national interest groups." Journal of Politics 32: 96-114.
STEINER, G. (1976) The Children's Cause. Washington, DC: Brookings Institution.
THURZ, D. (1971) "The arsenal of social action strategies." Social Work 16: 27-34.

Chapter 7

SHARPENING ADVOCACY SKILLS

BACKGROUND AND ASSUMPTIONS

All political advocates need to continuously improve their interpersonal and writing skills. Three of the most frequently mentioned areas of frustration for political advocates are working with committees composed mostly of elected people, preparing written documents for decision makers, and deciding upon which lobbying strategy to use. Political advocates are required to master all three kinds of situations. Most policy advocates probably spend anywhere from 50% to 90% of their working day performing tasks associated with committees, document preparation, and lobbying.

STOP AND THINK

How important are these tasks? Look at your appointment book for the past month. Which of these tasks takes up most of your time? The least amount of your time?

CONCEPTS AND ILLUSTRATIONS

COMMITTEE MANAGEMENT

There is a basic strategy that should be followed in working with committees composed primarily of elected people. This is the case regardless of whether the political advocate is presenting a case to the committee, a member of it, or has responsibility for setting it up and running some of its meetings. *Elected representatives must be dealt with differently depending upon the nature of the committee meeting and circumstances.* For example, if the meeting is a more *informal* one where the media and their constituents are not present, then you need to give them your "bottom line," your "hard sell," your basic argument. They need to understand specifically the political consequences of not supporting your position. You should allow them to ask as many questions as possible. Your responses should be candid and frank.

Alternatively, if the meeting is a formal one where it is open to the public (such as a hearing, council meeting, or other regularly scheduled meeting), then you must stay within your time limits, make your recommendations clear, and make your presentation short and to the point. But, more important, you must not embarrass or be too frank with members in public forums because you may hurt them politically. Leave that approach for the informal meetings. Elected people will appreciate this. *The message is to use the hard sell behind the scenes but give them the soft sell in public.* There are also some other " Dos" and " Don'ts" associated with how you present yourself in formal meetings.

Dos	Don'ts
Be prepared to make a presentation like a dramatist, technician, and pragmatist. Then, given the one to fit the audience, present one of the three.	Play over your head with people, only promise what you can deliver.
	Push too hard, they want subtle hustle.
Reflect style and dress of audience.	Embarrass in front of media or constituents.
Be patient and allow non-germane questions, then move on.	Let frustration surface, be calm and cool.
	Stick to a canned presentation, deviate to accommodate audience.
Make critical points in informal meetings or ahead of time.	

Some other useful tips related to committee management can be organized into scheduling, the content of written material presented to the committee, and the mechanics of running a meeting.

For *scheduling,* follow these guidelines:

(1) Pay attention to amenities like comfortable chairs, ventilation, refreshments, pencils, and so on.

(2) Only invite people at the same political level, they want to be around peers.

(3) Invite time-pressed people first, then build the schedule around them.

(4) Do not start meeting until important people arrive, delay if necessary.

(5) Always leave one hour more than advertised, meetings generally run long.

(6) Send written material two weeks before meeting and then a summary of it the day before.

(7) Call the day of meeting to remind their staff that the meeting is still scheduled.

For preparation of *written material,* follow these guidelines:

(1) Make it simple/brief.

(2) Make only recommendations something can be done about.

(3) Organize document so it is easy to access, to get in and out of.

(4) Separate your recommendations from description and analysis.

(5) Make sure recommendations are clear and not counterintuitive to the decision maker.

For the mechanics of *managing a committee,* follow these guidelines:

(1) Follow a five-minute rule, allow nongermane comments for no more than this.

(2) Formal meetings are largely symbolic, real work is done in executive sessions, so make it smooth; but do not push too hard.

(3) Allow meetings to run over within reason.

(4) Be prepared to call emergency, follow-up meetings.

(5) Do not require formal, recorded votes unless absolutely necessary.

EXERCISE

Run the following simulation game. Its purpose is to contrast formal versus informal meetings. The debriefing period after the game is over should stress the differences between formal and informal settings.

SIMULATION OF A
COUNTY BOARD OF COMMISSIONER'S MEETING

I. *SETTING*

Alcoa is a diverse, urbanized, and industrialized county in a midwestern state. In the last 10 years, the county has experienced serious economic and social problems. The unemployment rate fluctuates between 9% and 14% depending on the status of the steel industry, the main employer. Crime rates, divorce rates, child abuse and neglect cases, spouse abuse cases, and so on all increase and decrease with the unemployment rate. One-third of county is rural, small town, and very conservative on taxes, budget, and policy issues (i.e., they are generally opposed to funding social service type programs). Approximately a third of county is urban and blue-collar with high percentages of minority groups. Their unemployment rate is high and the need for social service programs is greatest. They are liberal on programs targeted to their area, but very conservative on tax and budget issues. The other third of the county is urban, but the residents are white middle to upper class. They are mixed toward the need for social service programs, but they can be convinced. However, they are very conservative on tax and budget issues. The board is composed of 10 members who represent distinct areas and geographic districts within the county.

II. *ISSUE AND TASK*

The Rainbow is a multiservice center (private, nonprofit) in the county. It provides a wide range of services (i.e., counseling, family therapy, career placement, child treatment, abortion counseling and family planning, consumer counseling for senior citizen housing, etc.). The Rainbow now has a budget of $5 million which is up from $1 million five years ago. It has grown fast and diversified in turn. On the one hand, it has visibility and credibility because of its range of programs. On the other hand, it is often criticized because it serves middle-class people and problems and does not target its programs efficiently and effectively. *The issue is that the Board of Commissioners (B.O.C.) must approve funding for next year for the Rainbow.* They are requesting $500,000 of the general revenue sharing and community development revenue sharing funds which the B.O.C. has the authority to allocate. Other groups want this money, too, since $500,000 represents 50% of the overall county funds available for service programs. The Rainbow cannot maintain its current services without the $500,000, so it has a vested interest in how the B.O.C. decides to allocate these funds. *There are two tasks necessary given this allocation issue.*

A. *Advisory Meeting* — Information gathering, informal meeting of 35 minutes. Executive Director of Rainbow makes brief presentation (5 minutes) advocating program continuation in all areas — total funding. Board members then informally question Director. No minutes are kept, no votes or decisions made, and no public input is allowed. This is an informal, executive session. Candid remarks and bottom-line questions are encouraged.

B. *Formal Hearing* — Decision time. B.O.C. allows the Rainbow 10 minutes to make its case in an open, public hearing before the board. Three staff of the Rainbow are available for the hearing and 15 minutes of follow-up questions by board. Chairman of B.O.C. runs meeting and sticks to formal agenda, time allotments, and so on. Vote on $500,000 request is necessary at end of hearing though board may table or ask for further information if it wants to. However, this would be a disaster to the Rainbow fiscally. They need a decision. If the $500,000 request is voted down, it must by prior agreement go back to the County Department of Social Services for further analysis. The board may not cut the budget request at this meeting. They must either approve or send back for another recommendation.

III. *ACTORS/PROFILES FOR SIMULATION*

Commissioners:

(1) *Ms. Lillian White,* 40, white middle-class, housewife, three teenagers, Independent, husband is executive with steel company, works part-time as volunteer with women's crisis center, sympathetic to Rainbow but cost-conscious and wants them to make their case for funds with facts and demonstrated needs. Has been known to storm out of meetings if commissioners get too political.

(2) *Chester Marcol,* 52, union job steward, black, factory worker who worked his way up in union hierarchy, Democrat, opinionated, represents Black community effectively. Does not like elaborate presentations and discussions. Wants to get to point. Impatient. Will filibuster if things do not go his way. Interested mainly in Drug Rehabilitation programs in black community.

(3) *Sander Phillips,* 45, small-town owner and operator of furniture business, very conservative Republican, generally opposed to service type programs. Politically very ambitious. Wants to run for

state-wide office. While conservative on fiscal and program issues, will listen if it is to his advantage.

(4) *Ester Walker,* 28, white, radical, organizer of food co-op in inner city neighborhood. Relates well to black community but disliked by middle class, white community, and people in rural areas. Adamant about women's rights and child abuse. Feels these are top priorities. Opinionated, dramatic, competitive, and a thorn in the side of anyone who does not agree with her. Has been known to tie up meetings with shouting debates for long periods of time.

(5) *Harry Sommers,* 41, calm, cool, collected, personnel manager for steel company, lives in standard middle-class area, swing voter that seems to vote in majority on all issues. Moderate on service and fiscal issues. Seems to like traditional, family, and counseling programs. Republican. Would like to hold another political office eventually.

(6) *Grayburn Rooster,* 47, farmer, Republican, fiscal conservative, anti-service programs, fundamentalist, cantankerous, wants to ignore urban part of county. Voted once for an adoption services program. Hard to move.

(7) *Gregory Smith,* 65, lives in small town, Independent, uninterested in service issues generally, low key, rarely talks, will listen if he thinks those talking are professionals, but generally quiet person who goes along with crowd.

(8) *Bonnie Radine,* 42, Ph.D., teaching at local university, teaches computer sciences and operations research, good analytical mind, votes Democratic but needs to be convinced. Very bright. Asks hard questions. Lives in fringe area around inner city. Considerable interest in planning and coordination issues.

(9) *Arturo Rangel,* 35, attorney for legal rights clinic in inner city, bright, probing, ambitious, Democratic, practical, pet interest in consumer rights counseling. Can be persuaded. Gets along well with others. Natural leader.

(10) *Ester Schwartz,* 42, MSW, Assistant Director for County Public Health unit in charge of health programs for teenagers. Knows service system in county well. Skeptical of nonprofit agencies. Stresses accountability issues, both fiscal and programmatic. Only service professional, moderate Democrat from middle-class area.

Game operator and two observers should begin debriefing but everyone should participate. Need 12 people to play.

DOCUMENT PREPARATION

Written documents that are used in the policy process come in many shapes and forms. Some are compendiums, others are brief and thin on background and analysis. Sometimes the decision-making situation and central actors demand certain kinds of documents, while other times it is unclear as to what kind of document would be the most helpful. In short, no standardly formatted type of document can be used under all circumstances. Rather, format and type should vary according to some of the critical attributes of the individual decision makers and the overall decision-making situation encountered.

There are a number of different kinds of policy documents, some of which should be introduced at different phases in the policy-making process. Advice givers[1] should not only take into account the time constraints and decision-making styles we discussed earlier *but they also should pay close attention to the various phases of the policy process and, more important, when and under what conditions the appropriate document will be used.* Advice must be carefully tailored to the intended audience(s), as well as decision-making situation if it is to be used.

Table 8 presents a simple typology of policy documents based on such characteristics as approximate length, use of data and analysis in the document, presentation of options and recommendations, intended audience, and potential use. The basic summary characteristics are helpful in understanding the kinds of things that get emphasized in each type of document and how, in turn, those things emphasized are connected to the intended audience, the anticipated impact, and the predominant decision-making style of the actors involved in the process. Another dimension of this typology is that certain kinds of documents are more likely to be produced in different work settings. For example, basic research is more likely to be produced outside of government and bureaucratic settings. Comprehensive analyses and Quick and Dirty memos are probably just as likely to be produced inside as well as outside government or bureaucratic settings. Policy options memoranda are largely indigenous to the government. Finally, think pieces could and do come from almost everywhere.

STOP AND THINK

When you have been involved in document preparation, which kind of document did you prepare most often? Are there characteristics other than those in Table 8 which describe the type of document you are most familiar with?

Table 9 allows one to move through the various phases (read from top to bottom along the left side of the table), while at the same time asking what the information-processing styles of decision makers are at each phase or step of the policy process.[2] Some kind of problem specification will occur in decision-making situations. The question is how will that occur? According to the decision-making styles discussed earlier, it would seem reasonable to expect that: the rational/ deliberative style would seek clear and concise quantification of the problem; the pragmatic/incremental would purposively leave the problem vague so that potential and future political support would not be lost at the earliest stages; and the emotional/ideological would seek a simple problem statement regardless of whether it was documented quantitatively.

There are a number of direct implications based on the kind of conceptualization presented in Table 9. First, the need for certain kinds and forms of information varies according to the phase or stage in the process. Second, the kind and form of information are also contingent upon the information processing of the decision makers involved. Third, it is possible, given the previous discussion on policy documents, to suggest that certain kinds of documents will be more helpful because they take into account more clearly the phase in the process and the type of decision-making style which is predominant. Therefore, one would be unlikely to bother with basic research if decision making was in the ratification and acceptance phase. In contrast, basic research may be more desirable and even necessary during the problem specification phase. And finally, the emotional/ ideological information processing style would probably have little or no use at all for basic research.

It is also important to emphasize that the people preparing policy documents may be very different, depending on what phase in the

(text continued on page 102)

TABLE 8 Types of Documents and Summary Characteristics

Type of Document	Approximate Length	Research Emphasis	Data Sources	Type of Data Analysis	Presentation of Options	Policy Conclusions or Recommendations	Primary Audience	Potential Impact or use	Decision-Making Styles Receptive to Document
Basic Research	100+ pages	Heavy and very sophisticated	Primary or original	High level statistics	Rarely	Rarely or very general	Academics Researchers Experts	Long term and conceptual	Rational/Deliberative
Comprehensive Analysis	80-100 pages, complete appendices	Heavy and very sophisticated	Primary or original emphasized but secondary will be used	High level statistics	Clearly delineated, exhaustive set	Very general, by implication	Academics Researchers Experts Policy analysts	Short term and conceptual	Rational/Deliberative, Pragmatic incremental
Think Piece	5-40 pages (varies considerably)	Light	Eclectic, whatever available	Minimal or nonexistent	Rarely	Very general by implication	Broad appeal, many audiences	Widespread, idea or concept is critical	All styles
Policy Options Memorandum	15-30 pages	Moderate	Secondary, use other reports, research	Simple statistics and graphics	Clearly delineated, but few of them	Very Specific, action orientation	Policy Analysts, Decision-Makers	Short term and Instrumental	Pragmatic/Incremental
Quick and Dirty Memo	1-10 pages	Moderate	Secondary, use other reports, research	Simple statistics and graphics	Occasionally but very general	Very specific, action orientation	Policy Analysts, Decision Makers	Short term and instrumental	Emotional/Ideological

Summary Characteristics of Document and Potential Use

TABLE 9 The Policy Process, Decision-Making Styles, and Policy Documents

Phases of the Policy Process	Decision Making Styles*		
	Rational/Deliberative (Analysis)	Pragmatic/Incremental (Feasibility)	Emotional/Ideological (Surprise or accidental action)
Problem Specification	Clear & concise quantification of problem B.R., C.A.	Problem purposively Left vague, quantification secondary T.P., B.R.	Clear and concise problem, but quantification not necessary Q.D., T.P.
Development and Structuring of Alternatives	Alternatives are exhaustive as possible and drawn heavily from research C.A.	Generation of only most feasible alternatives whether previous research or not P.O., Q.D.	Emergency or crisis demands quick solutions or fixes, little time for discussion of alternatives T.P., Q.D.
Ratification and Acceptance	Based on explicit weighting of criteria that are used to evaluate alternatives C.A., P.O.	Extraordinary bargaining and negotiation over long time P.O., Q.D., T.P.	Brief, often dramatic debate, quick decisions over short period of time Q.D., T.P.
Implementation: Planning & Design	Comprehensive design and planning process to be used to guide implementation C.A.	Test or pilot quickly and let experience accumulate over time P.O.	After thought - get moving as soon as possible so results can be shown Q.D., T.P.

TABLE 9 continued

Phases of the Policy Process	Decision Making Styles*		
	Rational/Deliberative (Analysis)	*Pragmatic/Incremental (Feasibility)*	*Emotional/Ideological (Surprise or accidental action)*
Evaluation, Assessment, Refurbishment	Based on careful, comprehensive & empirical assessment process --------- B.R.	Based on the amount and intensity of political support for policy/program --------- P.O.	Policy or program changes when crisis or system breakdown occurs - then quick fix adopted --------- T.P., Q.D.
Examples of Arenas	Space program Macro-monetary policy	Race relations Civil Rights Affirmative Action	Poverty programs of 1960's
Implications for Strategy	The appeal to objective need - must make empirical case, draw heavily on research, theory, and written documentation	The appeal to feasibility - appeal to broad enough coalition of support in a way that everyone gets a piece of the action	The appeal to values or emotions - timing is crucial, appealing to critical values

*Potential types of documents that would be helpful and useful are illustrated below the dotted line in each cell of the table:

B.R. - Basic Research
C.A. - Comprehensive Analysis
T.P. - Think Piece
P.O. - Policy Options Memorandum
Q.D. - Quick and Dirty Memo

process you are in. On the one hand, high-level staffs in the bureaucracy, congressional staffs, and lobbyists may all be preparing some kind of document during the ratification and acceptance stage, but they may have virtually nothing to do with the earliest stages of evaluation unless there is a public outcry or crisis. On the other hand, midlevel staffs in the bureaucracy, consultants, institutes, researchers in universities, and so on will play a more central role during the beginning of the evaluation phase.

Time is another important dimension in this discussion because some stages in the process seem to drag along in many policy areas, while in other areas the urgency or crisis-oriented nature of the issues demands rapid movement through the earliest phases. In this context, the choice of policy document (i.e., Quick and Dirty vs. comprehensive analysis) should be based to a great degree on the ability to respond to the time constraint given personal or organizational resources and their limitations.

History is relevant here as well, because in some policy areas like unemployment there is a long-established tradition of presenting updated, aggregate unemployment statistics in the policy debates. In other areas like abortion, policy statistics and research seem less important or secondary to the moral values and beliefs held by those involved in the debates.

Many more examples could be used to illustrate all of the connections between phase, style, and type of document. Table 9 is a graphic way of portraying these connections. If the stages of the policy process are understood more clearly and the predominant decision-making styles of the key actors at each phase are diagnosed accurately, then the choice of an appropriate policy document can be made more effectively and efficiently. The advice to the advice giver is to do your homework before writing or preparing a document. Otherwise, many personal and organizational resources will be wasted. With luck, this attention will minimize the kinds of frustrations created when documents are not read, are misinterpreted, or are lost on purpose.

At this point, the conceptualization introduced has indicated that at each phase in the policy process there may be somewhat different time constraints, different ways of processing information by decision makers, different people giving the advice, and different historical experiences with the presentation of advice. The last consideration to be examined is — when a single phase or the entire process is being looked at, the nature of the decision-making process itself can be analyzed and connected to the preparation of documents. Regardless of the other factors influencing more widespread utilization of policy documents, it is important to ask whether consensus, conflict, ambivalence, or some other combination of decision-making parameters exist. The importance lies primarily in the fact that while individual decision makers may differ widely in how they process information (and the advice giver may seek to adapt his/her advice accordingly), the larger decision-making situation or circumstances may dictate a different strategy of advice giving when multiple audiences are taken into account. It becomes a question of whether the advice giver has a single audience in mind, multiple audiences in mind, or just enough audiences to produce an operating majority (in a decision-making sense)? The nature of decision making itself at each stage (or all stages cumulatively) can reveal to the advice giver whether their documents are being prepared and designed in a way that takes into account the broader needs of the decision-making situation.

Table 10 categorizes the nature of decision making into highly conflictual, highly consensual, no clear preferences, and fluctuating. Over time, a policy area may exhibit all of these, *but the critical point is that the advice giver must be able, at any one point in time, to diagnose the overall decision-making situation.* So, for example, focusing on the agenda and whether or not it is fixed, rapidly changing, or unclear allows one to provide somewhat different kinds of advice. The most complex situation is the fluctuating one where everything seems volatile and in a state of transition, so that it is unclear as to what types of advice would be the most helpful. The novice advice giver would, no doubt, find this situation disconcerting. The other three situations are easier to describe; and correspondingly, it is easier to tailor advice to meet the overall needs of these situations.

A careful examination of Table 10 should link up with the discussion heretofore. Consensual decision making makes immediate action possible and the need for careful analysis, documentation, and bargaining less necessary. Policy documents which raise the consciousness of otherwise predisposed decision makers are right on target. Alternatively, comprehensive analysis seems appreciated and desirable when no clear preferences are present. Other interpretations like this are made easily from Table 10. It could be said, therefore, that depending on the nature of the decision-making situation, all

TABLE 10   Nature of Decision Making and Choice of Policy Documents

| | *Nature of Decision Making (Selected Characteristics)* | *Document Choice* | |
		Type of Policy Document Recommended	*Primary Emphasis In Document*
Highly Conflictual	agenda set priorities established but they are different most decision makers' positions known external support for options clear coalitions formed *feasible options debated, considerable bargaining	Policy options memorandum Quick & Dirty Memo Occasionally Think Piece	feasibility of options or recommendations
Highly Consensual	agenda set priorities established, little disagreement most decision makers' positions known external support & much pressure coalitions unnecessary, mobilization needed *debate limited, dramaturgy stressed	Quick & Dirty Memo Think Piece	immediate action next steps, or consciousness raising
No Clear Preferences	agenda unclear priorities unclear decision makers ambivalent, disinterested, and uninformed external support & pressure just beginning no coaltions *discussion based around acquiring information of all types	Basic Research Comprehensive Analysis	methodological adequacy or providing comprehensive information
Fluctuating	agenda changing rapidly priorities fluctuating decision makers formulating positions external support & pressure substantial coaltion formation taking place *discussion based around acquiring most convincing information	all of above	all of above

*Critical aspect of decision making situation.

the different types of policy documents mentioned could serve a useful purpose. More broadly, it could also be said that, in a functional sense, policy documents serve different needs. Given a particular decision-making situation, a predominant information-processing style, and a certain phase in the policy process, there are policy formats which are more optimal to the circumstances and, therefore, more helpful. However, the reoccurring theme developed in this discussion has been that a more theoretical and conceptual (opposed to an incremental and anecdotal) approach to the preparation of documents can lead to increased and more widespread use of the advice givers documents in the long run.

STOP AND THINK

Recall the last two or three frustrating decision-making situations you either observed or participated in. How close did these situations come to the ones described in Table 10? Were you aware of how you presented information in these situations?

EXERCISE

Select three policy documents you have prepared or have been involved in preparing over the last year. Evaluate the extent to which you considered format, decision-making styles of the audience, and the nature of the decision-making process when you prepared these documents. Having done this, indicate how the documents could be prepared differently now (given the discussion in this section).

LOBBYING

Lobbying can be separated into three activity areas: making direct contacts with decision makers, trying to reach them indirectly through intermediaries, and keeping the channels of communication open so that access is maintained over time. These activities are the ones practiced by most successful lobbyists. The generalization most frequently heard by lobbyists is that direct personal communication is the most effective activity when it is possible. No matter what, careful assessment of resources, both personal and organizational, should be made before a major strategy is designed. Many lobbying activities require large amounts of effort and yet are just not effective. Experienced, skilled lobbyists do not do all of the tasks in Table 11 equally. They allocate their time to be effective, but also efficient. Many conventional lobbying activities are just a waste of time. It is vital to continuously reassess what works and what does not. For example, constituent mail works with some legislators, but not others. Some legislators would be offended by being offered direct campaign support, but others would require it as a price for helping you or your organization.

Often legislators encourage formal testimony and written communication, while others want informal and verbal presentations of your position. In short, the savvy political advocate must learn how to rapidly diagnose individual decision makers (and situations) and then put together a reasonable lobbying strategy based on resource availability. In fact, many argue that lobbying is more an art than a science because successful lobbying tactics are so hard to identify and appear to be connected so closely with the personal style of the lobbyist or his/her organization.

STOP AND THINK

When you lobby, what tactics do you use most frequently? Which of these tactics are generally successful? Unsuccessful? How often do you evaluate your tactics to determine whether they are worth using again?

The best advice to those political advocates who seek to become better lobbyists is to continuously reassess your strategy. Make sure you are adapting your strategy to fit the individual decision maker (do not use the same strategy over and over again) and decision-making situation. Observe other lobbyists so that new and creative ideas can be incorporated into your strategy. And do not ignore the fact that decision makers are people with human needs and motivations; they are not just politicians seeking reelection. Your case must be presented in a way that is reasonable, yet persuasive. *Finally, do not*

TABLE 11   Selected Lobbying Activities

A. Direct Personal Communication
   1. Personal presentation of arguments
   2. Presentation of research results
   3. Testifying at hearings

B. Communication Through Intermediaries
   1. Constituency
   2. Friends
   3. Experts
   4. Letters/telegrams
   5. Public relations
   6. Publicize voting records

C. Opening Channels of Communication and Keeping Them Open
   1. Entertaining
   2. Bribery
   3. Contribute money and time to campaign
   4. Collaborate with other groups

forget that lobbying is reciprocal. If you want something, you should be prepared to give something.

One of the frequent complaints of decision makers is that advocacy groups are always asking for something but they rarely, if at all, offer something that the decision makers want — even if that is something as simple as respect or courtesy.

EXERCISE

Keep a log for one month as it relates to your lobbying activities. Estimate times spent in each of the three activity areas illustrated in Table 11. Critically assess time allocation and draft a new lobbying strategy for the next month. This is a good exercise for an entire staff or agency board to complete.

Have each participant identify at least one successful and one unsuccessful lobbying strategy that he or she has used in the past. The discussion leader should look for similarities and differences across these examples. Then ask participants to redo unsuccessful strategies. Use the three activity areas mentioned in Table 11 to organize the discussion.

NOTES

1. As in Chapter 6, "advice givers" is used to refer to political advocates who are performing the advice-giving function when preparing documents.

2. Refer to Chapter 6 for a discussion of the information-processing styles of decision makers.

REFERENCES

DLUHY, M. (1980) "Muddling through or thinking about the problem seriously — how to prepare policy documents, present information to decision makers, and maximize the impact of your advice," in J. Tropman et al. (ed.) Effective Meetings: Improving Group Decision Making. Beverly Hills, CA: Sage.

MELTSNER, A. (1979) "Don't slight communication: Some problems of analytical practice," Policy Analysis 5: 367-392.

TROPMAN, J. E. (1980) Effective Meetings: Improving Group Decision Making. Beverly Hills, CA: Sage.

TROPMAN, J. E., H. R. JOHNSON, and E. J. TROPMAN (1979) The Essentials of Committee Management. Chicago: Nelson-Hall.

WEBER, J. (1975) Managing the Board of Directors. New York: The Greater New York Fund.

Chapter 8

CONCLUSION

In the first chapter I raised the question of what it would take to become a more successful political advocate for disadvantaged groups. My argument has been that the response to this question is two-fold. *First,* the political advocate needs a clear and I hope realistic orientation toward social change. Chapter 1 discusses various orientations toward change that can be taken and their consequences. At a minimum the successful political advocate needs to be able to take a step back from his/her day-to-day activities and be able to develop an orientation toward change that will guide his or her behavior and activity in the future. Without such an orientation, you might find yourself continuously changing your behavior without having any insight into what you are doing and why you are doing it. Among other things, this contributes to "burn out," frustration, and the wasting of precious personal and organizational resources.

The lack of such an orientation may also mean that some political advocates will continue to do the same thing over and over again since they basically have little insight into their behavior. Here the problem is one of rigidity and the inability to change behavior to accommodate to the situation. The political advocate who has a clear orientation toward social change suffers from neither of these limitations. In short, the "committed political advocate" has an institutional reform orientation toward social change and he or she uses it regularly to evaluate his or her own behavior and activity. This orientation is in back of everything they do.

TABLE 12   Summary of Chapters (The X's represent those chapters which emphasize particular elements of the framework)

Framework and Its Elements	Chapters				
	3 Clarifying Issues and Underlying Values	4 Policy Development Process	5 Assessing Decision Maker Needs and Choosing an Effective Advocacy Role	6 Coalition Building	7 Sharpening Interpersonal and Written Skills
Appeal to Objective Need		X	X		X
Value Manipulation	X	X	X		X
Designing Policy for Target Groups	X	X		X	
Building Organizational Support Policy		X		X	X

Chapter 1 argues that when one takes the institutional reform orientation toward social change, the probability of achieving success for disadvantaged groups is the greatest. While the other three orientations may not benefit disadvantaged groups as much, it may be better to have one of them than to have no orientation at all or to be unaware of your orientation.

The *second* response to the question of how to become a more successful political advocate is that a proactive stance toward policy and the political process on a regular and ongoing basis is needed. Chapter 2 identifies a framework that can be used to help achieve this more proactive stance. The framework identifies key elements that must be considered before a successful strategy to affect policy is developed. All of the elements in the framework should at least be considered ahead of time, even if only some of the elements are actually selected and used in practice.

Table 12 summarizes the connections between the framework presented in Chapter 2 and the rest of the book. For example, if the decision is made to stress value manipulation in your political strategy, then you should carefully review Chapters 3, 4, 5, and 7. On the other hand, if the decision is made to emphasize the appeal to objective need, then Chapters 4, 5, and 7 should be reviewed. Of course, if all the elements of the framework are to be used, then all the chapters should be reviewed. A proactive stance toward policy therefore requires considerable knowledge about the political process and its operation. Chapters 3 through 7 provide this detailed knowledge. In this sense, the acquisition of this knowledge will lead to more understanding, less bewilderment, less alienation, and, ultimately, more confidence for the political advocate. This confidence will contribute immensely to success in achieving your policy objectives.

This volume is written for practitioners. Clarifying your orientation toward social change and using the framework will not be easy. This material will help you to develop your strategy. You will want to stray from the material in this volume. Keep following it. Do not stop until you are confident that you have the best strategy. Change your strategy when necessary; update it periodically; try it out on sympathetic audiences; and keep at it. The challenge of helping disadvantaged groups in a modern, rapidly changing society demands it.

Glossary

1. Access

people or groups who seek to modify or change policies toward youth must have *access* to the decision makers who have the power to make these kinds of changes. *Access* in this context, means, first, locating these decision makers and, second, establishing a relationship with them so that at a later point in time people or groups seeking change can make their case or argument to these decision makers. Before influence can be exerted by people and groups interested in changing policies toward disadvantaged groups, these people and groups must have *access* to the appropriate decision makers who have the power to change policy.

2. Advocate

means to represent in a political sense the interests of disadvantaged groups. *Advocating* the interests of disadvantaged groups therefore includes all of those activities aimed at changing policies affecting them. An *advocate* is a person who perceives of him/herself as representing the interests of disadvantaged groups in the policy process.

3. Broker

when there is a decision-making situation where there is conflict and a stalemate among the major actors involved, some person or persons play the role of bringing the various sides together by offering compromise solutions to decision-making problems. The art of bringing the various and opposing actors together is known as brokering. The broker is therefore a person who is capable of playing that role in complex decision-making situations.

4. Bureaucracy

large-scale, public organizations which are given the major responsibility for implementing various policies or programs affecting youth. These organizations are primarily run by civil servants and may be found at the national, state, and local level.

5. Clientele

the people and groups who are the major beneficiaries of policies and programs for disadvantaged groups. For example, youth directly served under the Runaway Youth Act are viewed as the clientele of that program.

6. Political Coalition

the banding together of separate groups and organizations to achieve a singular political objective. The coalition exists only to achieve political objectives. When those objectives are achieved or the groups or organizations no longer have an interest in banding together, the coalition goes out of existence.

7. Constituency

elected political representatives look at the people or groups who live in their state or district as constituents. All those people who geographically live in their state or district are thought of as their constituents.

8. Dramatist

various kinds of people give advice or make their case to decision makers concerning youth problems and their solutions. The *Dramatist* is a person who gives advice and makes his/her case in a certain way. For example, the *Dramatist* is very effective at appealing to the values of decision makers. Additionally, the *Dramatist* tends to present one-sided advice or arguments which dramatize the plight of youth and their problems. Most of the activities of *Dramatists* are aimed at raising the consciousness level of decision makers by appealing to shared values (see definitions of Pragmatist and Technician for alternative forms of advice giving).

9. Ideology

the set of values that a person has about how the political system operates and should operate and how it ought to respond to problems of youth. Three basic ideologies (radical, liberal, and conservative) are distinguished according to their contrasting views of the political system, the problems generated in that system, and the range of solutions that are appropriate. The radical basically wants to restructure the political system and its major institutions and processes. The liberal wants only to marginally change the system and its institutions and process. The conservative wants to basically leave the system and its institutions and processes alone and instead change individuals and their behavior.

10. Implementation

the process of designing, carrying out, and monitoring the activities necessary to make sure that the policy and program objectives are achieved and realized.

11. Jargon

professional program managers in government, politicians, local agency directors, and lobbyists in the youth area use a vocabulary or set of terms which people outside of their circles do not understand. They use either highly technical language that few other people understand or "buzz words" which the average lay-person has never heard before. To dejargonize is therefore to simplify the vocabulary and language that professionals use when interacting with the general public.

12. Methodology

the research design and procedures used by analysts to generate information and data to answer policy questions.

13. Network

to network is to establish communication linkages between individuals and groups interested in changing policies toward youth. A network has been established when these linkages are regular and ongoing opposed to sporadic and infrequent.

14. Proactive

to take the initiative in the policy process by putting forth recommendations for change, pressing for their adoption and implementation, and monitoring the policy process to make sure that the changes have been made. *Proactive* advocates do not wait for changes to come from others, rather they are the initiators of such change.

15. Pragmatist

various kinds of people give advice or make their case to decision makers concerning youth problems and their solutions. The *Pragmatist* is a person who gives advice and makes his/her case in a certain way. For example, the *Pragmatist* is very concerned with pointing out the feasibility of his/her recommendations. Since the *Pragmatist* is interested in making sure that change does occur no matter what its magnitude, he/she is careful to point out to decision makers the consequences of inaction (see the definition of Technician and Dramatist for alternative forms of advice giving).

16. Policy

a set of decisions made over a long period of time which are aimed at achieving certain, narrow objectives. *Aging policy,* for example, is a set of decisions aimed at achieving objectives relating to aging. Thus aging policy at the national level may be to discourage poverty. There are many decisions that have been made over time which are aimed at achieving that policy objective.

17. Policy Development

the activities aimed at establishing, clarifying, and formally drafting policy objectives (especially as they relate to disadvantaged groups).

18. Political Process

the formal and informal decision-making steps that must be cleared before a policy becomes adopted. Thus, a sequence of steps, each requiring consensus or approval, must be followed before a policy change becomes a reality.

19. Rationalistic

a way in which people make decisions. They clarify and rank their goals, array a set of alternative choices, assess these choices based on their goals, and make a choice after completing the assessment.

20. Social Change   the objective change in the living situation of an individual or group. The noneconomic changes in living situations such as family structure, educational opportunities, and environmental surroundings are illustrative of social as opposed to economic changes.

21. Strategy   the art of deciding how to manage your activities and behavior in a way that will cause others to modify their policy position in the direction you are moving.

22. Technician   various kinds of people give advice or make their case to decision makers concerning problems and their solutions. The *Technician* is a person who gives advice and makes his/her case in a certain way. For example, the *Technician* is skilled at presenting comprehensive analyses of data and information in a way that will convince decision makers to act in a certain way. Most of the emphasis by the *Technician* is on the logic of the analysis and the recommendations and whether they are connected to data or scientific evidence (see the definitions of Pragmatists and Dramatist for alternative forms of advice giving).

About the Author

MILAN J. DLUHY is Associate Professor in the School of Social Work and Lecturer in Political Science at the University of Michigan. He has written extensively in the areas of social welfare policy; programs for the elderly and youth; housing; and urban problems. He has also held positions with both federal and state governments. He currently serves as a consultant to a number of advocacy groups.